A History
of the
Chateaugay Ore and Iron Company

Compiled by
J. R. Linney

A facsimile of the 1934 edition

TEACH Services, Inc.
Brushton, New York
2008

PRINTED IN
THE UNITED STATES OF AMERICA

World rights reserved. This book or any portion thereof may not be copied or reproduced in any form or manner whatever, except as provided by law, without the written permission of the publisher, except by a reviewer who may quote brief passages in a review. The author assumes full responsibility for the accuracy of all facts and quotations as cited in this book.

This book was written to provide accurate and authoritative information in regard to the subject matter covered. It is sold with the understanding that the publisher is not engaged in giving legal, accounting, medical or other professional advice. If legal advice or other professional expert assistance is required, the reader should seek a competent professional person.

2008 09 10 11 12 13 14 · 5 4 3 2 1

Copyright © 2008 TEACH Services, Inc.
ISBN-13: 978-1-57258-571-3
ISBN-10: 1-57258-571-4
Library of Congress Control Number: 2008932473

Front cover: Train depot at Lyon Mountain, NY

Back Cover: A vertical view of a mineshaft in the Lyon Mountain mine
Photo by Timothy Hullquist, 2007

Published by

TEACH Services, Inc.
www.TEACHServices.com

The Delaware and Hudson Railroad

BOARD *of* DIRECTORS

INSPECTION *of* LINES : :

JUNE 7th to JUNE 10th, 1934

LEONOR F. LOREE
President
Chateaugay Ore and Iron Company

PHOTO BY BLANK-STOLLER, INC.

A
History of
the
Chateaugay Ore and Iron Company

Preface

This year's annual inspection trip of the Board of Directors of The Delaware and Hudson Railroad Corporation includes an inspection of the plant and operations of the Chateaugay Ore and Iron Company, a subsidiary of The Delaware and Hudson Company and a substantial contributor of freight traffic to The Delaware and Hudson Railroad.

It seemed appropriate, therefore, that this history of the Chateaugay Ore and Iron Company, which was compiled by Mr. J. R. Linney, Vice President, should be prepared for the information of the Board and for the preservation of a record of the Company's activities.

F. W. LEAMY.

Office of Senior Vice President,
Chateaugay Ore and Iron Company,
32 Nassau Street, New York,
June 1, 1934.

Table of Contents

	PAGE
PREFACE	5
TABLE OF CONTENTS	6
LIST OF ILLUSTRATIONS	8
INTRODUCTORY	11

CHAPTER I

EXCERPTS.   Etymology; The First Mentioned Ironworker; Iron, The Master Metal; The Iron Master 13

CHAPTER II

HISTORY OF THE CHATEAUGAY ORE AND IRON COMPANY.   Weed and Williams; Land Grants; Early Owners; Discovery of the Chateaugay Ore Bed; Early Prospecting, Incorporation of the Chateaugay Iron Company; Early Mining and Concentration; Catalan Forges at Russia and Belmont; Charcoal Consumption; Early Transportation; Chateaugay Iron in Brooklyn Bridge; Hardships in the Early Period; The Chateaugay Railroad; Increasing Production in the Early '80's; Williamstown (Standish), its Early Development; "81" Mine; The First Forge at Williamstown (Standish); Incorporation of the Chateaugay Ore and Iron Company; Identification of The Delaware and Hudson Company with Chateaugay Ore and Iron Company; Mining in the '80's; Blast Furnace Built at Standish; Removing Catalan Forge from Belmont to Standish; The Ball and Norton Electro-Magnetic Separator; American Bloomery goes out of Existence; The Delaware and Hudson Company takes over control of the Chateaugay Ore and Iron Company; Supplanting narrow Gauge of Railroad with Standard Gauge; Replacing Steam with Electricity; Coke takes the place of Charcoal in Standish Furnace; The New President; Scientific Study and Development of the Chateaugay Properties, including Magnetrometric and Geological Surveys; The Sinking of No. 1 Shaft; War Period; Post War Development, including Sintering Plant, New Concentrating Plant, and Modernization of Standish Blast Furnace 19

CHAPTER III

GEOLOGY.   Composition of Chateaugay Ore; Formation of Chateaugay Ore Bed; Faults, dikes and folds in the Ore Body and their effect on Mining; Ore Reserves 65

Table of Contents — Concluded

PAGE

CHAPTER IV

MINING AND MANUFACTURING CHATEAUGAY PRODUCTS. Mining Methods; Milling and Concentration; Sintering; Smelting; The Foundry.................................... 71

CHAPTER V

SALES AND DISTRIBUTION OF CHATEAUGAY PRODUCTS. Chateaugay's Products; Sale of Lump Ore; Concentrates in the Blast Furnace and Steel Industry; Sintered Ore as a Sweetener; Chateaugay Pig and its unlimited uses in Foundries and Steel Mills; Chateaugay Pig supplants Charcoal Iron; The inherent qualities of Chateaugay Iron; The Electronic theory of fatigued Castings; Iron Ore Tailings and their uses; Greenman's Report; Total Sales of Ore Tailings, 1925 to 1933; Woodlands products; Future prospects in the Woodlands Department........................ 109

CHAPTER VI

WOODLANDS AND FORESTS. Relation of Forests to Development of the Adirondacks; Forest Land Purchases and the reasons for Acquisition of such Properties; Wood converted to Charcoal; Sale of Pulpwood to the Glens Falls Paper Mill Company, later known as the International Pulp and Paper Company; Destructive Forest Fires; Sherrard's Forest Survey in 1904; Forest Tree Nurseries; White Pine Blister Rust; Forest Tree Plantations; 1918 Timber Survey; Cornell University Timber Cruise in 1920 and 1921; Property Acquisitions; Boundary Surveys; Conditions Existing in Reforested Areas........................ 127

APPENDIX

CHRONOLOGY OF IRON AND STEEL (IN PART). Prehistoric Times; Earliest Historical Period; Christian Era; Mediaeval Period; Renaissance Period; Early Historical Period; Colonial Period; Revolutionary Period; Period of Scientific Development; Civil War Period; The Steel Age; The Twentieth Century; Northern New York State Area 141

List of Illustrations

	PAGE
Leonor F. Loree, President	Frontispiece
Andrew Williams and Smith M. Weed, founders of the Chateaugay Ore and Iron Co.	20
Mining Ore, Open Pit, Chateaugay Vein, 1878	24
Lyon Mountain, 1880, showing Old Plank Road	26
Chateaugay Lake transportation route between Chateaugay Ore Bed and Iron Works in early period	28
Steamboat "Maggie" on Chateaugay Lake, 1880	29
Flume at Outlet Chateaugay Lake, furnishing power for Forges, 1880	30
Water Wheel at Forge at Outlet Chateaugay Lake, 1880	32
Tools used in Chateaugay's Catalan Forge, 1880	33
Catalan Forge of 20 Fires, Chateaugay Lake, 1880	34
Charcoal Kilns, Chateaugay Lake, 1880	35
Sanderson Co. is now a part of Crucible Steel Co. and still a Chateaugay customer	36
Fighting Snow, Chateaugay R. R. 1880	38
Chateaugay Passenger Train, Lyon Mountain, 1880	39
Narrow Gauge Locomotive, Chateaugay R. R., 1880	40
Shop, Lyon Mountain, 1880	42
Separator, Lyon Mountain, 1880	43
Forge and Iron Works, Williamsburg (now Standish), 1881	44
Trip Hammer Operation, Standish, 1882	46
Log Houses, Lyon Mountain, 1885	47
Chateaugay Company's Offices, Plattsburg, 1885	48
Chateaugay R. R. Train, 1887	49
Standish Furnace, 1886	50
Chateaugay Separator, Lyon Mountain, 1890	52
Charcoal Furnace and Catalan Forge at Standish, Chateaugay Ore and Iron Co., 1895	53
Separator, Lyon Mountain, 1907	54
Lyon Mountain, 1907	56
Large Pillar, Old Workings, Chateaugay Mine, 1920	57
Present Chateaugay Shop, Lyon Mountain	58
Present Standish Furnace	60
Present Power House, Lyon Mountain	61
20 foot Snow Drift, Lyon Mountain, 1924	62
Map showing the areal distribution of principal rock formations in the Adrondacks, Etc.	64

List of Illustrations—Continued

	PAGE
Model of Chateaugay Mine. White indicates Mined Area, black indicates Ore intact	66
Sample Section of 750 foot level, No. 4 East Drift	68
Present Headframe, Hoist House and Change House, No. 1 Shaft, Chateaugay Mine	70
Section along Main Hoisting Shaft, Chateaugay Mine	72
Drifting on Vein, Chateaugay Mine, 1933	74
Stoping Ore, Chateaugay Mine, 1933	75
Ore Chute, bottom of Stope, Chateaugay Mine	76
Drill Sharpening Shop, present Chateaugay Mine	78
Storage Battery Locomotive and Ore Train, Chateaugay Mine, 1933	79
Electric Hoist. No. 1 Shaft, present Chateaugay Mine	80
Large Quintiplex Pump in present Chateaugay Mine	82
Heavy Timber on Main Drift Lower Levels, Chateaugay Mine, 1933	83
Main Haulage Way showing Timbered Section, Chateaugay Mine	84
Present Chateaugay Concentrating Plant, Lyon Mountain	86
Present Control Room, Concentrating Plant, Lyon Mountain	87
Pulley Type Magnetic Separators for Cobbing Rock out of the Ore	88
A Battery of Vibrating Screens, present Chateaugay Concentrating Plant	90
Latest Improved Type Drum Magnetic Separator used in Chateaugay Concentrating Plant	91
Magnetic Separators, present Chateaugay Concentrating Plant	92
Graph showing Per Cent Iron in Concentrates and Man Hours per Ton Concentrates from 1906 to 1933	94
Present Chateaugay Sintering Plant, Lyon Mountain	95
Interior view of present Chateaugay Sintering Plant	96
Chateaugay Sintered Ore as it goes to R. R. Cars	98
Standish Furnace, 1933	99
Standish Blast Furnace, 1934	100
Flow Sheet from Raw Materials to Finished Steel Products	102
Casting Molten Iron. Standish Furnace, 1933	103
Present Standish Blast Furnace	104
Chateaugay Ore & Iron Company Burden Sheet, Standish Blast Furnace	106
Per Cent Items of Cost, Chateaugay Pig Iron	108
Award for Quality, World's Fair, 1893	110
States and Foreign Countries into which Chateaugay Iron is shipped	112
George Washington Bridge, Hudson River, N. Y. City. 15,000 tons Chateaugay Iron used to manufacture the Steel Cables	114
Dam on Saranac River, built with Chateaugay Ore Tailings	116
New York State Concrete Highway, built with Chateaugay Ore Tailings	117
Section of D. & H. R. R. Track near Bluff Point, ballasted with Chateaugay Ore Tailings	118
Underpass D. & H. R. R. Chateaugay Ore Tailings used to make the Concrete	119
Hydro Electric Power Plant on Saranac River, built with Ore Tailings	120

List of Illustrations — Concluded

	PAGE
Interior Power House, Saranac River, built with Ore Tailings	121
36 inch Belt Conveyor carrying Ore Tailings to R. R. Cars for market	122
Concrete Highway Approach to Overhead Crossing, D. & H. R. R. Whitehall. Tunnel and Grade Elimination, built with Chateaugay Ore Tailings	123
Whitehall Tunnel and Grade Elimination, D. & H. R. R., built with Chateaugay Ore Tailings	124
Seed Beds and Transplants of various species and ages at Bluff Point Nursery in 1921	132
Type of Areas Denuded by Forest Fires at Wolf Pond in Franklin County. Foreground Reforested in 1915 with Scotch Pine. 1910 Scotch Pine Plantation in Background	133
A view of the 1910 Scotch Pine Plantation at Middle Kilns in Franklin County, photographed in 1915. Alder Swamp in foreground along Middle Kiln Brook	134
Photograph taken in 1915 of the Northerly portion of the 1910 Scotch Pine Plantation South of Wolf Pond in the Salmon River Valley	136
A view of the 1912 Scotch Pine Plantation at Wolf Pond in Franklin County established under a small growth of Poplar and Cherry as photographed in 1915	137
1915 Red Pine Plantation South of Wolf Pond in Franklin County	138
Ore Separator in the Adirondacks, early part of 19th Century	166
Rolling Mills in the Adirondacks, middle part of 19th Century	168
Bowen and Signor's Iron Works, Saranac, N. Y., 1871. The Ore Bed now owned by Chateaugay	172
Three-Pipe Bloomery Forge at Belmont, N. Y. Typical of Forges used in early part of 19th Century	174
Wooden Trip Hammer used at Belmont, N. Y.	176

Introductory

The history of the Chateaugay Ore and Iron Company is a story of an "ironworks" that was founded, among others, in the dense wilderness of the Adirondack Mountains, in New York State, about three quarters of a century ago. Adventure and romance filled many of the years of its pioneer founders and builders.

Not only the survival, but the steady growth of the Company, is due to, more than any other one thing, the exceptional quality of its iron ore, which is conceded to be the best found on the American Continent, and possibly in the world.

The President of the Company, as early as the year 1907, recognized the possibility of this iron ore becoming a large source of freight revenue to The Delaware and Hudson Railroad. Its location, near the northerly end of the railroad, added to the attractiveness of the traffic, because the ore and iron, on the way to the steel producing centers, could be carried in coal cars, many of which would otherwise be hauled empty southward.

Exploration work was begun and carried on for several years to determine the extent of this ore body, which was followed, with the exception of the war period, by extensive development and improvement in plant and equipment. Now being most modern and up-to-date, this plant has sufficient capacity to maintain, and because of the high quality of its product does maintain, a foremost position in the markets.

The Chateaugay Ore and Iron Company has, in normal times, proven to be self-sustaining, as well as being a large contributor of freight to the railroad. It has great possibilities for the future, and some day the freight movement of its products southward, including those of its vast acreage of woodlands which have been reforested with many millions of pine trees, many of which are approaching commercial maturity, may even surpass the anthracite movement northward.

Chapter I

EXCERPTS

Etymology

The word "iron" originally came from the old Teutonic language group, and was represented in the early branches of that group about as follows: Anglo-Saxon, iren, yren, isen and irsern; Old Saxon, isarn; Old High German, isarn, isan, isen; Middle High German, isen; Dutch, ysen; Gothic, eisarn; Icelandic, jarn; Danish and Swedish, jern. The word may possibly have a distant relationship to the Latin "ferrum."

The word "steel" is from a root with no Latin representative, but came from the Teutonic language group. The Anglo-Saxon representative forms were: stel, stele, style, cognate with the Dutch staal; Icelandic, stal; Danish, staal; Swedish, stal; Old High German, stahal.

The First Mentioned Ironworker

Tubal-cain, who was seven generations from Adam, was a forger of every cutting instrument of brass and iron.

(Genesis iv, 22)

Iron, the Master Metal

A little thought will clearly indicate that iron is as vital to modern civilization as air and water are to life. It has become so common, however, that like air and water its true importance is lost sight of by most people. No other metal has contributed so much to the welfare and comfort of man. There is scarcely an article used in our daily lives that has not been produced from iron, or by means of it.

Take, for example, the bread that we eat. Ploughs turn the soil, harrows level it, drills sow the seed, machines harvest the wheat and thrash it. Rolls crush the grain to separate the flour. Engines bring the flour over the railroads to our homes, where it is made into dough in pans and baked in a stove. Finally, the bread is sliced from the loaf with a knife. All of these instruments are products of iron.

The Ironmaster

There is a legend connected with the building of Solomon's temple, the truth of which we have no reason to doubt. It is substantially this:

When the magnificent structure, which required the genius and skill of the most expert workmen, was approaching completion, the wise king determined to manifest his appreciation of the successful efforts of all engaged in its construction by tendering to them a banquet within its walls. Upon a given day, all labor was suspended, and in response to the king's bidding, all the workers in gold, in silver, in brass, in iron, in stone, and in timber, assembled in holiday attire to partake of the king's bounty. The wise man passed from guest to guest, while they were seated around the richly ladened table, and with pleasant words and kind interrogatories he won their confidence and confirmed their respect and love.

Of one he asked, "What trade is yours, and how do you aid in the great work?"

"I am a hewer of stone," replied the man, "and I help provide for the massive foundations and the temple walls."

"And whence came the tools with which you work?" asked the king.

"From the ironmaster, Sire; he made my tools."

Of another the king asked, "What work is yours, my man?"

"I am a worker in wood," quoth he, " and I fashion the cedar and fir and algum tree."

Again the king queried, "Who made the tools with which you so skillfully work?"

"The ironmaster, O King, made all my tools."

And so from mason to carpenter, to the cunning worker in gold, in silver and brass, to the graver of gravings, to each in turn came the king, and from each he learned the same story, that the ironmaster made the implements.

At last the king came to the ironmaster himself, and queried again, "What trade is yours, good man; and how do you help at the temple?"

"I am the ironmaster," responded he, "and I made and shaped the iron for the temple, and made the tools for the other craftsmen, and keep them in repair."

"Aye," quoth the king, "but who made the tools with which you work?"

"I made my own tools," replied he.

Whereupon, the wise man proclaimed that the ironmaster, having made his own material, and his own tools, as well as the tools of the other workmen, was the king of all craftsmen.

Chapter II

HISTORY OF THE CHATEAUGAY ORE AND IRON COMPANY

ANDREW WILLIAMS AND SMITH M. WEED, FOUNDERS OF THE CHATEAUGAY ORE AND IRON CO.

History of the Chateaugay Ore and Iron Company

The beginning of the development of the Chateaugay Ore and Iron Company is closely connected with the early iron industry, which was of considerable importance to northern New York during most of the Nineteenth Century, and especially to Clinton and Essex counties which, 54 years ago, produced 23 per cent of the total iron ore output of the United States.

From 1798, when Platt erected the first forge on the Saranac River at Plattsburg, N. Y., the iron business took on impetus. Year after year new ore deposits were discovered and ironworks started. The Saranac River, due to its many rapids and falls, lent itself very profitably as a source of power in many places. Its proximity to abundance of charcoaling timber and to numerous ore beds made it ideal for ironworks locations, of which several operated successfully for many years. Thus, this section of northern New York was destined to become a large and important part of the American Bloomery.

Closely associated with this industry were two men, Andrew Williams and Smith M. Weed, the founders of the Chateaugay Ore and Iron Company, and this narrative would not be complete without making brief mention of some of the activities of these two gentlemen.

Andrew Williams, when a young man, began work at one of the Catalan forges on the Saranac River. Having a good common school education to begin with, he applied himself diligently year after year until he became one of the best informed and most able men in the industry, always endeavoring to improve the quality of his iron, continually prospecting and seeking purer and better ore deposits.

Several years before the opening of the Chateaugay Ore Beds, it is said that Mr. Williams had secured samples of this ore, packed it many miles through the forests to his forge on the Saranac River, and made up special samples of iron from it, which were properly ear-marked as they went to the trade, the customer being requested to report back as to the quality. The splendid reports received from various customers in the trade on the samples of iron made from the Chateaugay ore and the many requests for more of it, caused Mr. Williams to become very much interested in the opening and development of the Chateaugay Ore Bed, despite its inaccessibility. It may be that he thought along the lines of Emerson's Mousetrap Story.* * * In any event, he associated himself with Smith M. Weed and, despite the many natural obstacles, undertook to open up this ore and make a better iron, and did so.

Smith M. Weed graduated from the Law School at Harvard University in 1857, and in 1859 he married Carrie L. Standish, a daughter of Colonel Matthew M. Standish, a lineal descendant of Colonel Miles Standish, of Plymouth. Standish, N. Y., where the Company's blast furnace is located, was named for Mrs. Weed's family.

Mr. Weed, in addition to being an able lawyer, was a statesman of first rank. He was elected and re-elected many times to the State Assembly, and made and retained the friendship and confidence of Governors and Presidents.

Mr. Weed, more than any other one man, was responsible for interesting the Delaware and Hudson Canal Company's officers in the building of a railroad between Whitehall and Plattsburg. The history of The Delaware and Hudson Company, "A Century of Progress," says of Mr. Weed:

" Early in 1872 he journeyed to New York in the effort to interest the Delaware and Hudson Canal Company. At a meeting with some of its officers and Managers, at which I. V. Baker who shared his aspirations was present, Mr. Weed readily convinced George Talbot Olyphant, acting as president in the absence of Mr. Dickson, LeGrand B. Cannon and others that such a line would be of great advantage to the company. Thereupon Mr. Weed drew from his pocket articles of association of The New York & Canada Railroad Company, already signed by several residents of Plattsburg and Clinton County. The remaining signatures necessary to effect its incorporation were quickly supplied."

In later years, the two gentlemen who successfully founded and commercially developed the Chateaugay Ore and Iron Company were known as Honorable Andrew Williams and Honorable Smith M. Weed, both having won distinction in State activities, as well as in the industrial enterprise in which they were interested; one a master of the industrial arts, and the other a master in the art of statesmanship; both of noble character.

In 1781, the Legislature of New York set apart, in the north central part of the state, a tract of land containing about 665,000 acres, lying in Clinton, Franklin and Essex counties, to satisfy the claims of two regiments of soldiers which the State of New York had found it necessary to raise to protect its frontier settlements from frequent pillage by the Indians and other enemies. Congress was too poor to furnish troops for their protection, and so the State sought to raise them and pay for their services in the manner above mentioned. This land is the so-called Old Military Tract.

---

* * * Many are inclined to credit Elbert Hubbard with the Mousetrap Story. Sarah Yule, in a book called "Borrowings," printed many years before the Roycrofters, credits Emerson as being the author of the quotation.

Due to failure of the act to express clearly its meaning, and because of its vagueness, another act was passed in 1786, defining the area to be surveyed, and allowing the speedy sale of these and other unappropriated lands within the state. However, no part of the Old Military Tract was ever awarded on bounty claims. It was ultimately all sold by the State as "wild lands." The Town of Dannemora, in which the Chateaugay Ore Bed is located, lies in Township No. 5 of this Old Military Tract.

In September, 1794, Township No. 5 became the property of William Henderson, merchant, of New York City, who sold it in January, 1795, to Jacob Mark. In February of the same year, Mark mortgaged it to Jacob and Robert Leroy, and from that time on, for about a quarter of a century, it being considered of little value, the property changed hands a number of times. In 1822, it was owned by John L. Norton and Hannah Murray, who divided it up into 300 lots which lay in what was afterwards incorporated into the towns of Ellenburg and Dannemora. In the apportionment of the 300 lots between the owners, the part which lay in Dannemora fell to Hannah Murray, who in turn conveyed it, on November 22, 1822, to Lloyd N. Rogers.

There is good reason for believing that the discovery of iron ore in the north central portion of this tract was made many years before. Several miles westward of the Chateaugay Mine, and on the same strike as the Chateaugay Ore Bed, is an old opening (81 mine), which had evidently been worked to a considerable extent at some remote period, a shaft having been sunk, from which quantities of waste which present day manufacturers would call good ore had been thrown out and left. Trees of considerable size had grown over some of this waste pile. It is reasonable to suppose that this is the so-called Prall vein, from which William Bailey, who erected a forge on the Chateaugay River about five miles below the outlet of Chateaugay Lake, in 1803, obtained his ore, shipping it on rafts or boats through the Upper and Lower Chateaugay lakes to his forge.

However, there does not seem to be any record of the actual discovery of the Chateaugay Ore Bed up to the time of Mr. Rogers' purchase. In the year 1823 the bed of ore, practically phosphorus free, now known as "Chateaugay," and which has been proven to be the best in the world, was supposed to have been discovered by an old trapper named Collins.

But the Ore Bed lay in the depths of what was then considered an almost impenetrable wilderness, and it was many years before any attempt was made to work it. Even after it was known, it excited little interest among capitalists, for the reason that it was so far from lines of transportation, and lying in a region which abounded in natural obstacles, held to be practically insurmountable against the building of roads of any kind.

It was not until about 1868 that the first steps were taken toward utilizing this treasure, when Messrs. Foote, Weed, Meade and Waldo made a contract with Edmund Law Rogers, of Baltimore, son of Lloyd N. Rogers, and soon after obtained possession of the property.

MINING ORE, OPEN PIT, CHATEAUGAY VEIN, 1878

However, for a period of about five years there was very little done in the way of development of this ore body. Small groups of men were engaged during the summer months in digging the ore, piling it on the surface to be loaded during the winter months and hauled by horse-drawn sleighs on the snow through the dense wilderness to the Catalan forges on the Saranac River.

The interest of the above named group was soon transferred to the Chateaugay Iron Company, organized by Smith M. Weed and Andrew Williams, and in the fall of 1873, the work of developing the property began in earnest. A plank road was built from the Saranac River Plank Road, branching from that road at Saranac Hollow, and running 13 miles through the mountains to the Ore Bed.

At this time there was only a small clearing in the dense forest, with a few log shanties, where the village of Lyon Mountain now stands. Its only tie to civilization was the newly constructed road to Russia, N. Y.

For a period of about four years the working of the ore was confined practically to the outcroppings, loading by hand directly into wagons; and as the pits became deeper, the sides were sloped on a grade which permitted the driving of the wagons on the floor of the Bed. However, this method soon became impractical. The ore was thereafter loaded into small cars, and hoisted to the surface by means of a whimsey, the power being supplied by horses. The ore was then transferred to wagons and hauled to the No. 1 Separator, which was located on the present site of the Delaware and Hudson's turntable, on the bank of Separator Brook at Lyon Mountain.

The No. 1 Separator consisted of roasting pits, stamps, and jigging baskets. The roasting pits were rectangular in shape, approximately thirty feet long, twelve feet wide, and ten feet high, enclosed on three sides by stones. Four-foot cord wood was placed in the pit to a height of about six feet, and then covered with three to four feet of lump ore. The wood was ignited and the ore roasted until the fire burned out. In the operation there were three of these pits to a unit; while the roasted ore was being taken from one pit, the second pit was roasting another batch, and the third was being prepared for still another. This represented a cycle, with a roasted batch of ore on hand at all times. The roasting of the ore made it easier to crush.

The ore from the roasting pits was then loaded into wagons and hauled to the stamps at the Separator. A stamp consisted of a heavy stick of timber, varying in length, hinged at one end and protected on the other by an iron plate. It was raised by means of an eccentric, and dropped by gravity on top of the ore until the material was crushed fine enough to pass through $\frac{1}{4}''$ opening.

The sizing apparatus consisted of iron bars, spaced $\frac{1}{4}''$ apart, located directly under the stamp and, as the ore was crushed, it passed through these bars and was then shoveled into the jigging baskets for concentration.

LYON MOUNTAIN, 1880, SHOWING OLD PLANK ROAD

The jigging baskets consisted of a screen in the shape of a cylinder open at the top, with a bail to which was attached a piece of wooden timber acting as a fulcrum or lever. The ore was shoveled into the basket, which was then lowered into a tank of water and "jigged" up and down. The ore, being heavier, sank to the bottom of the basket, while the rock impurities formed a layer on the top, which was scraped off and sent to the waste pile.

The operation was continuous 24 hours daily, except Sunday, producing approximately ten gross tons of concentrated iron ore, containing about 55 per cent iron. The loss of iron in the tailings, however, was enormous. The concentrated ore was then loaded into wagons, which held approximately two tons, and transported over the plank road to Russia, N. Y., where it was made into blooms in the six-fire forge owned by Andrew Williams and C. F. Norton.

In the subsequent years, the property was opened up considerably. The mines were sunk deeper, necessitating larger hoisting equipment and also the introduction of pumping machinery to take care of water drainage. Up until this time, all of the drilling was done by hand, using jumpers and hammers, two men drilling on the average twelve lineal feet per shift. With the introduction of compressed air driven drilling machines, the drilling and the tonnage per man per day was substantially increased. A steam sawmill was built and kept in constant operation, turning out lumber for new buildings, plank roads, etc. An addition was made to the separator to take care of the increased output of the mines. Additional miners and mill hands were brought in, until the total number of employed reached about 150. This, of course, meant that new houses had to be built, and at this time we find about 40 houses, a school house and church composing the village of Lyon Mountain.

A small dam on Separator Brook, which comes brawling down from Mount Lyon, secured a head of 48 feet, which was sufficient to run the separator a good portion of the year, and a 30 horse power steam engine supplied whatever force was lacking for either the separator or sawmill. The Chateaugay Ore and Iron Company now owned over 35,000 acres of land in this immediate region, a great portion of which was covered with heavy timber, well adapted to lumbering and charcoaling purposes. They also had a 40-year lease on 4,000 additional acres on which the Ore Bed was located, and with the privilege of cutting every tree which grew upon it. Thus, it will be seen that they had control of nearly 40,000 acres of land, with a large supply of iron ore under it and plenty of charcoaling timber on its surface.

With the increasing of men and machinery the output of concentrated ore reached approximately 50 gross tons per day, containing about 55 per cent iron. This was loaded into wagons and hauled over a splendid plank road to the dock on Upper Chateaugay Lake. Here it was transferred into barges, which were towed to the Company's forge fires at Belmont, at the outlet of Lower Chateaugay Lake, by the Company's steamer, "Maggie," named after Miss Maggie Weed (daughter of Hon. Smith M. Weed).

CHATEAUGAY LAKE TRANSPORTATION ROUTE BETWEEN CHATEAUGAY ORE BED
AND IRON WORKS IN EARLY PERIOD

STEAMBOAT "MAGGIE" ON CHATEAUGAY LAKE, 1880

FLUME AT OUTLET CHATEAUGAY LAKE, FURNISHING POWER FOR FORGES, 1880

The "Maggie" was 28½ feet long over all, with an 11 foot beam, drawing four feet of water. It was driven at the rate of ten miles per hour, by a 25 horse power steam engine. The barge, the "Iron Age," was 80 feet long and 17 feet wide, and carried approximately 150 tons of ore. After the ore was transported to its destination, it was transferred by hand to a small car which was drawn by a cable to the stock piles at the forges.

At the outlet of Chateaugay Lake, at Belmont, ground was broken for the erection of a dam and ironworks, in the year 1874, and operations began in January of the following year. The entire operations were driven by water power under a head of 18 feet. The "mill pond" was 12 miles long, both Upper and Lower Chateaugay Lakes having been raised by the dam about 4½ feet. All the wood, coal and ore were moved on the Lake in barges and rafts by the "Maggie." Each Fall before the close of navigation, enough ore was stored at Belmont to run the forges through the Winter. There were ten first-class fires, which were increased in later years to 20, the largest Catalan forge in operation in the country, if not in the world, at that time.

The forge turned out approximately 15 gross tons of half blooms per day, which the Company found no necessity for piling up, being almost constantly behind in their orders, due to the exceptional quality of the iron and the tremendous demand for it. The consumption of charcoal was approximately 2,500 bushels per day. The Company also owned and operated a sawmill at this location.

The blooms and billets were hauled by wagons and sleighs to Chateaugay, N. Y., and shipped via the Ogdensburg & Lake Champlain Railroad to the steel districts of Pennsylvania and Ohio. There is no doubt but that the same inherent qualities of the Chateaugay iron, which are in demand by the steel men of today for their toughest projects, were known and appreciated during this period. The records at this time indicate a large tonnage of Chateaugay blooms being made for shipment to the wire manufacturers for the Brooklyn Bridge.

The Catalan forge furnace, in which iron was made direct from ore, was an open hearth, about 2½ feet by 3½ feet, with a stack 20 feet to 25 feet high for carrying off the gases.

The blast of air was usually furnished either by a bellows, or by means of a trompe. The pipe that carried the air to the hearth was coiled in the stack of the furnace, the object being to preheat the blast of air, which resulted in a saving of fuel.

The operation consisted of a charcoal fire, stimulated by a blast of air, iron ore and charcoal in small quantities being added alternately by the bloomsmen, who also regulated and adjusted the fire, until the batch of iron, called a "loupe," weighing about 300 pounds, was made. This usually took about three hours.

WATER WHEEL AT FORGE, AT OUTLET CHATEAUGAY LAKE, 1880

TOOLS USED IN CHATEAUGAY'S CATALAN FORGE, 1880

CATALAN FORGE OF 20 FIRES, CHATEAUGAY LAKE, 1880

CHARCOAL KILNS, CHATEAUGAY LAKE, 1880

CENTRAL VERMONT
RAILROAD LINE.

J. W. HOBART, Gen'l Manager.   E. A. CHITTENDEN, Sup't Local Freight Traffic.

GEO CASSILY, Ass't Sup't Local Freight Traffic.

This Bill of Lading is from _____ to _____
The rate of freight through from _____ to _____
is _____ per 100 lbs.   Advanced charges _____
Via _____ Line.

No. _____   Freight Office Chateaugay, N.Y. Sept 26 1892

RECEIVED OF Chat. Ore & I. Co. the following described packages in apparent good order (condition and contents not known) consigned as marked and numbered in the margin, which we promise to transport (subject to the exceptions below) over the line of this Railroad, to its Freight Station at its terminus, and deliver in like good order to the consignee or owner, or to such Company (if the same are to be forwarded beyond the limits of this Railroad), whose line may be considered a part of the route to the place of destination of said goods or packages; it being distinctly understood that the responsibility of this Railroad as a common carrier shall cease at the station where such goods are delivered to such persons or carrier; but it guarantees on its part and on the part of other companies that the rate of freight for the transportation of said packages shall be as above specified.

PROVIDED, That no Carrier or Company forming a part of the line over which said freight is to be transported will be responsible for demurrage...

LOADED IN NYC 2461   CAR No. _____

MARKS AND CONSIGNEES	ARTICLES	WEIGHT
Sanderson Bros Steel Co. Syracuse N.Y.	316 Billets Iron	29155

CONDITIONS AND RULES.

[fine print conditions follow]

D. R. Chapman

SANDERSON CO. IS NOW A PART OF CRUCIBLE STEEL CO. AND STILL A CHATEAUGAY CUSTOMER

The "loupe," in a pasty state, mixed with slag, was loosened in the hearth by means of bars, and then lifted from the furnace with tongs, known as "grampuses," promptly taken to the trip hammer and forged into blooms or billets, a bar of iron about 5 inches square, varying in lengths from two to six feet, depending upon the market demands.

The iron made was exceptionally pure. The following is an analysis made recently in the Company's laboratory of one of the old Chateaugay blooms which has been preserved:

Iron	99.70%
Silicon	.08
Sulphur	.017
Phosphorus	.017
Combined Carbon	.130
Manganese	Nil

The Company at this time was fairly prosperous. The following was told of the late Hon. John Moffitt, who for a number of years was President of the Plattsburg National Bank & Trust Company:

> "It seems that in the early '70s Mr. Moffitt was General Manager of the Chateaugay Company's operations. His responsibilities as Manager included the purchase of the Company's supplies, the payment of bills, the sale of products, and the collection of all money due the Company. Shortly after the close of one successful year, the Company having manufactured and sold some 4,000 tons of iron, the late Hon. Smith M. Weed, President of the Company, asked Mr. Moffitt how much money the Company made during the past year. The reply represented a very substantial profit. Mr. Weed promptly said that he had been to see the bookkeeper, and was quite sure that the books did not show net earnings anywhere near this amount. Mr. Moffitt promptly replied that he did not care what the books showed. He had paid all of his bills and had that much money left in the bank."

This early period of development, however, was accompanied by a great deal of hardship for both the management and the employees. The winters were cold, with heavy snows, making it very difficult at times to obtain food and clothing. Wild meat, in the form of venison, rabbits, birds and fish, was quite plentiful and, had it not been for this, there would have been a great deal more suffering than there was. Flour, one of the necessities of these hard laboring pioneers, was lacking for months at a time, and was obtained, when possible, at a premium.

Late in the '70s, the Company realized that in order to develop properly the rich resources of its property to the best advantage, it must secure railroad communication with the great iron markets of the country. The question was, which way should it strike out from the mine, lying in the very

FIGHTING SNOW, CHATEAUGAY R. R., 1880

CHATEAUGAY PASSENGER TRAIN, LYON MOUNTAIN, 1880

NARROW GAUGE LOCOMOTIVE, CHATEAUGAY R. R., 1880

heart of the wilderness. Two routes were open to it: One down the Chateaugay valley to Chateaugay, N. Y., connecting with the Ogdensburg and Lake Champlain Railroad, and the other to Dannemora, to connect with the Plattsburg & Dannemora line. In February, 1879, when the snow was four feet deep in the woods, the work of making a preliminary survey was commenced, and early in the spring the following data were at hand: Distance to Chateaugay, 17 miles, an almost straight line, with an easy grade all the way, and the line running nearly half way through the Company's own land, past its Catalan forge at Belmont, and the other half through a fine farming country, from which considerable local traffic would be derived. Distance to Dannemora, 17 miles, ten of which lay through solid wilderness, a crooked line running around two mountains and alternately toward all points of the compass; a hard line to grade, with the promise of little local traffic. Everything seemed to indicate the selection of the Chateaugay route as the most natural, cheapest and best.

However, Thomas Dickson, President of the Delaware and Hudson Canal Company, a close friend of Smith M. Weed, concluded that the proper movement of this ore was to Plattsburg, then via the New York and Canada Railroad. On the 20th of May, 1879, the Chateaugay Railroad was organized, with Thomas Dickson as its President. Subsequently, the lease of the Plattsburg and Dannemora Railroad was secured from the State, and about the 5th of June the contract was let for grading of the Chateaugay Railroad from Dannemora to the Ore Bed. On the 8th of June the work began, and on December 6th the track laying was finished to the first shaft. On the 17th of December, the first regular train ran over the entire line, and on December 18, 1879, the first train of ore was moved to Plattsburg.

In the subsequent years, the operations at Lyon Mountain spread out and increased at a rapid rate. Directly above the "Old Opening" shaft, where the first blow was struck toward developing the Chateaugay Ore Bed in 1867, and continuing southwest along the strike of the vein, the Williams Opening shaft had been sunk to a depth of approximately 200 feet. Between the shafts was an engine house, 36 x 52 feet, housing a compressor for air drills, and pumping and hoisting apparatus for both shafts.

Farther along was the railroad station, a building which now contains the offices of the present Company, and directly across the tracks a building 40 x 50 feet, with two stalls for housing locomotives, had been erected. Adjoining this was the machine shop, 36 x 65 feet, with a second story for a carpenter shop. This department contained the most up-to-date iron lathes, planers, drills, and other tools needed to repair or rebuild engines or machinery, or to do car repair work.

On the east bank of Separator Brook, an engine house 40 x 50 feet, housing a 200 horse power engine, designed to drive the separator, tools in the

SHOP, LYON MOUNTAIN, 1880

SEPARATOR, LYON MOUNTAIN, 1880

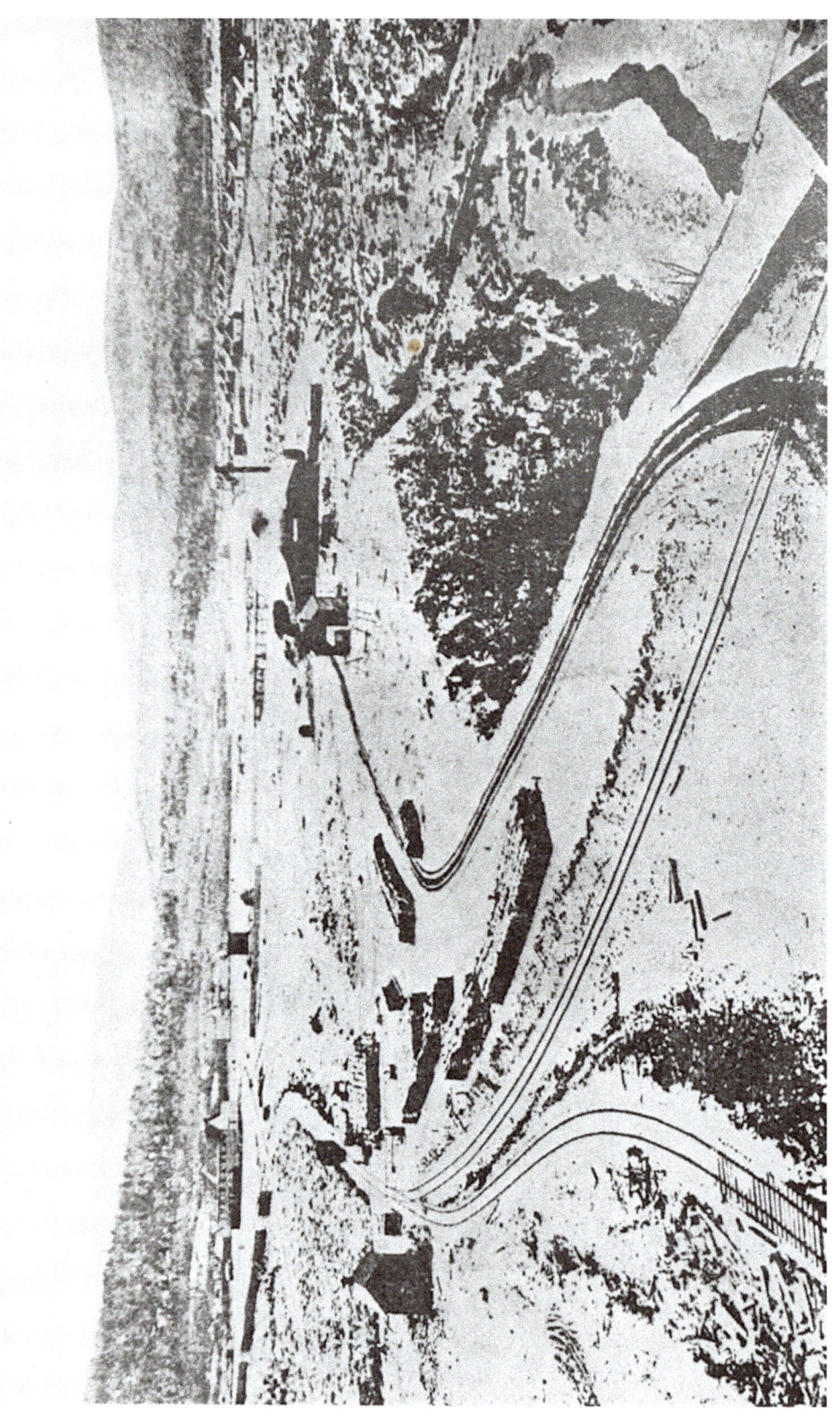

FORGE AND IRON WORKS, WILLIAMSTOWN (NOW STANDISH), 1881

machine shop, and hoisting apparatus, was erected. On the opposite side of the brook was No. 2 Separator, 40 x 60 feet. Above, on the slope, were the roasting kilns, alongside of which was a side track from which ore from all shafts, to be separated, was dumped directly into the kilns, and thence worked down to the ground floor of the building, which was furnished with a Blake jaw crusher and a revolving Conkling separator. A short distance above was a substantial dam. Cars were loaded direct from the separator and hoisted by an engine on an elevated track to the main track.

At this time the vein was uncovered for about 1,500 feet. Shafts had been sunk at numerous locations west of No. 2 Separator and were equipped with up-to-date steam hoisting apparatus, steam pumps, and steam-driven compressors for the air drills. The average width of the vein was 20 to 25 feet, the depth unknown.

About 1880 the Company re-opened the 81 mine, which was located a short distance east of Williamstown (now Standish), to supply ore to the forges located on the Saranac River, at Clayburg, a distance of approximately 11 miles. A separator containing the latest types of roasting, stamping, screening and jigging equipment was built on the brook. The concentrated ore from the mill was loaded into wagons and hauled over a plank road, which had been recently built for that purpose, to Clayburg. However, within a year, the forges and equipment were moved to Williamstown (Standish), and in 1881 the first forge began operations near the site of the Company's present modern blast furnace.

The new location was ideal, for it was in the heart of what seemed to be an almost endless supply of wood for charcoal, and only four miles from the terminus of the Chateaugay Railroad.

In this same year, 1881, the Chateaugay Ore and Iron Company was incorporated, and purchased the properties of the Chateaugay Ore Company, the Chateaugay Iron Company, a furnace at Plattsburg, and the Chateaugay Railroad Company. The Delaware and Hudson Canal Company became closely identified with the new Company at this time.

By 1883 the mines and mills were producing concentrated ore for some 60 forges in Clinton and Essex counties. At Belmont, 20 forge fires were running, the largest Catalan forge in the country, besides a six-fire forge at Standish, and a charcoal blast furnace at Plattsburg. Lyon Mountain had grown from a few shacks in the wilderness to a thriving community of some 3,000 inhabitants, the busiest spot in Clinton county. Nearly a million dollars had been expended in the purchase of machinery and equipment, for even then those dauntless pioneers, Williams and Weed, realized the wealth and future possibilities which lay in this wonderful bed of iron ore.

Improved mining methods and machinery were constantly being introduced, and as the market demanded it, the output was rapidly increased. This,

TRIP HAMMER OPERATION, STANDISH, 1882

LOG HOUSES, LYON MOUNTAIN, 1885

CHATEAUGAY COMPANY'S OFFICES, PLATTSBURG, 1885

CHATEAUGAY R. R. TRAIN, 1887

STANDISH FURNACE. 1886

of course, necessitated a like increase in milling capacity. As a result, new mills were erected at strategic points on the most convenient brook.

Just below the Williams Pit, No. 3 Separator, with roasting, stamping and jigging equipment, was built, and at Bradley Pond outlet, No. 4 Separator, complete with all equipment, was erected to handle the ore from Parkhurst Shaft. Every ton of ore was immediately turned into iron which, it seems, was rapidly marketed.

The method of mining at this time, which was continued for some years, was to sink shafts on the dip of the vein to a depth of about 300 feet, and at intervals, along the strike (i. e., the general longitudinal direction of the vein) of about 250 feet. Levels were opened into the ore on both sides of each shaft every 50 feet, leaving a small pillar to protect the shaft. After the ore was blasted, it was loaded into wheelbarrows, wheeled out to the shaft, dumped into the skip and hoisted to the surface. The rich lump ore was sorted out by hand on the surface, and shipped direct to the steel mills for use in the open hearth and puddling furnaces.

As the demand and production of iron increased, so it was with the consumption of charcoal, and in the ensuing years it became necessary to tap still further the forests in order to obtain an adequate supply of wood for the making of charcoal. In the year 1885, the Company began the erection of a blast furnace at Standish, extending the railroad from Lyon Mountain to that point, and later to Loon Lake, as a part of its plant facility, in order to reach the furnace, charcoal kilns and woodlands that it owned.

In the year 1886, the Catalan forges at Standish were temporarily abandoned, and the making of pig iron commenced in the new blast furnace, using charcoal as fuel. This resulted in the development of an entirely new market for this product, pig iron being an entirely different product from bloom iron produced by the Catalan forges. However, steel making by the Bessemer process was gaining by leaps and bounds in this country, and the Chateaugay Iron, being extremely low in phosphorus, was in great demand. Many additional houses, a merchandising store, a school house and a church sprang up in the village, and Standish began to make industrial history.

The Company continued to make pig iron at Standish, and bloom iron at Belmont, until the year 1893. The major depression of that period having gotten well underway by this time, the Company, in order to consolidate its operations at one point and close to its railroad, moved the forges from Belmont to Standish, so that both bloom iron and pig iron could be made at that point and shipped to market by rail.

The slump in the iron business continued for several years, due to the depression, and when the revival of industrial activity began to show itself in the late '90s, there came a great demand for the ore, as well as the iron. A comparatively new device for separating the ore came into the market about this time,

CHATEAUGAY SEPARATOR, LYON MOUNTAIN, 1890

CHATEAUGAY ORE AND IRON CO., 1895
CHARCOAL FURNACE AND CATALAN FORGE AT STANDISH.

SEPARATOR, LYON MOUNTAIN, 1907

known as the Ball and Norton Magnetic Separator. With this machine, it was possible to make a concentrate running 60 per cent iron, with a tailing of only 7 per cent iron, at the rate of ten tons per hour per machine. The separator at Lyon Mountain was enlarged, and a number of these machines installed, with very good results.

As steel making by the Bessemer process, and wrought iron making by the puddling process, increased, the demand for Catalan forge blooms decreased, not on account of quality, but because these new processes could make wrought iron and steel which would serve the purpose at the time for less than half the cost of Catalan forge blooms. As a result, the American Bloomery, which for many years had been the backbone of the iron and steel industry of the country, was doomed.

The Company subsequently abandoned its Catalan forge operations and continued making low phosphorus pig iron in the blast furnace, using charcoal as fuel, and also continued to ship concentrates and lump ore from its mines at Lyon Mountain.

By now, it was obvious that the Chateaugay Ore Beds were very extensive, this having been proven by openings on the outcroppings for a distance of several miles, and to a considerable depth, all of the ore being of the same character and purity. Because of the exceptional quality of the ore and the iron, the demand continued to increase, and it became evident that the property should be operated on a much larger scale.

At this time, The Delaware and Hudson Company had a considerable financial interest in the Chateaugay Ore and Iron Company. After having a study of the property made, President Willcox, of The Delaware and Hudson Company, recommended to its Board of Managers that they take over the Chateaugay Company and operate it. On July 29, 1903, the Board of Managers of The Delaware and Hudson Company authorized that procedure.

The narrow gauge railroad, which meanwhile had been extended to Lake Placid, was promptly supplanted by a substantial, standard gauge road. At the same time, wherever possible, grades and curvature were reduced to make possible the heavy movements of iron ore which were contemplated from the property, and which subsequently took place.

A large steam power plant was built, and two 500 K. W. electrical generators were installed to furnish electric power for the electric motors, which were installed in place of steam-driven engines, at isolated points, and also for additional electro-magnetic separators. There were also installed two Laidlaw Dunn air compressors, to insure an ample supply of compressed air for the drilling machines in the mine.

Because of the tremendous amount of charcoal used by the blast furnace, the increasing difficulty of securing a sufficient supply, and the fact that by this

LYON MOUNTAIN, 1907

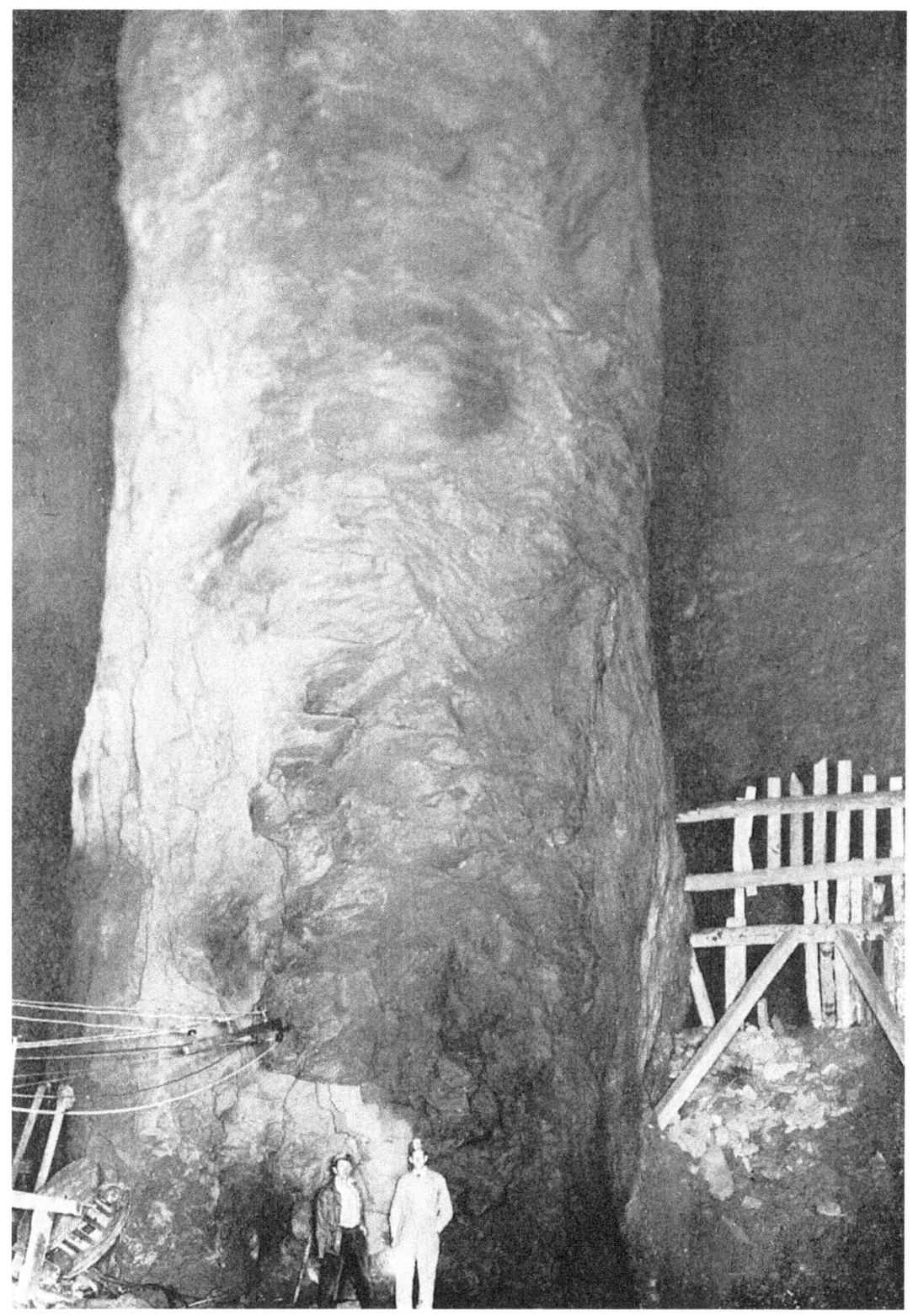

LARGE PILLAR, OLD WORKINGS, CHATEAUGAY MINE, 1920

PRESENT CHATEAUGAY SHOP, LYON MOUNTAIN

time coke had replaced charcoal in most of the blast furnaces in the country, and could be secured at a much lower cost, the Standish Furnace was changed from a charcoal to a coke furnace.

Between the years 1903 and 1907, a great deal was done in the way of replacing much of the light equipment with heavier and more substantial equipment. The output of ore and pig iron was considerably increased.

Then, in 1907, came the new President, Mr. L. F. Loree, with many years of scientific engineering and practical experience behind him. A new separator, which was badly needed, was completed in this year, equipped with the latest improved magnetic separators, crushing and screening equipment, and did excellent work. Unfortunately, it was destroyed by fire the following year, which made it necessary to use the old No. 2 Separator, which had been closed down.

A well defined plan of study of the property was immediately put into action by the President. This included a magnetometric and geological survey, diamond drilling, chemical analyses, and surveying and mapping the mine workings. The results of this study revealed that the Chateaugay Ore beds were tremendous in size, containing an almost endless supply of iron ore, practically free from Sulphur and Phosphorus.

It took several years to complete the above mentioned exploration work, during which time the Company's mines and blast furnace operated continually. In 1914, plans were made for the development of the ore body on a large scale, which included a new hoisting shaft, to be 1,600 feet deep, with steel headframe and modern electrically-driven hoisting equipment.

This work was well under way, and the shaft down 900 feet, when the demands for Chateaugay iron and iron ore became so great, on account of the war, that it was necessary to postpone the development work, in order to concentrate all activities on production.

In 1917, it became necessary to build a new separator, because the old No. 2 Separator was beginning to fail badly, on account of the many years it had been standing. The new separator was completed and put in operation by the fall of 1918.

In 1919, when the demands of the war had eased up considerably, it was decided to proceed with the development of the mine. The No. 1 Shaft, which had been sunk to a depth of 900 feet, was extended to a depth of 1,685 feet, with four compartments; one for pipe and ladderways, one for men and supplies, and two for hoisting ore, all enclosed in steel and concrete.

Levels were opened east and west on the strike of the vein, at intervals varying from 150 feet to 300 feet, depending on the nature and character of the vein. Stopes were opened up, and electric locomotives installed, and by 1924 all of the mining operations were confined to the new No. 1 Shaft.

PRESENT STANDISH FURNACE

PRESENT POWER HOUSE, LYON MOUNTAIN

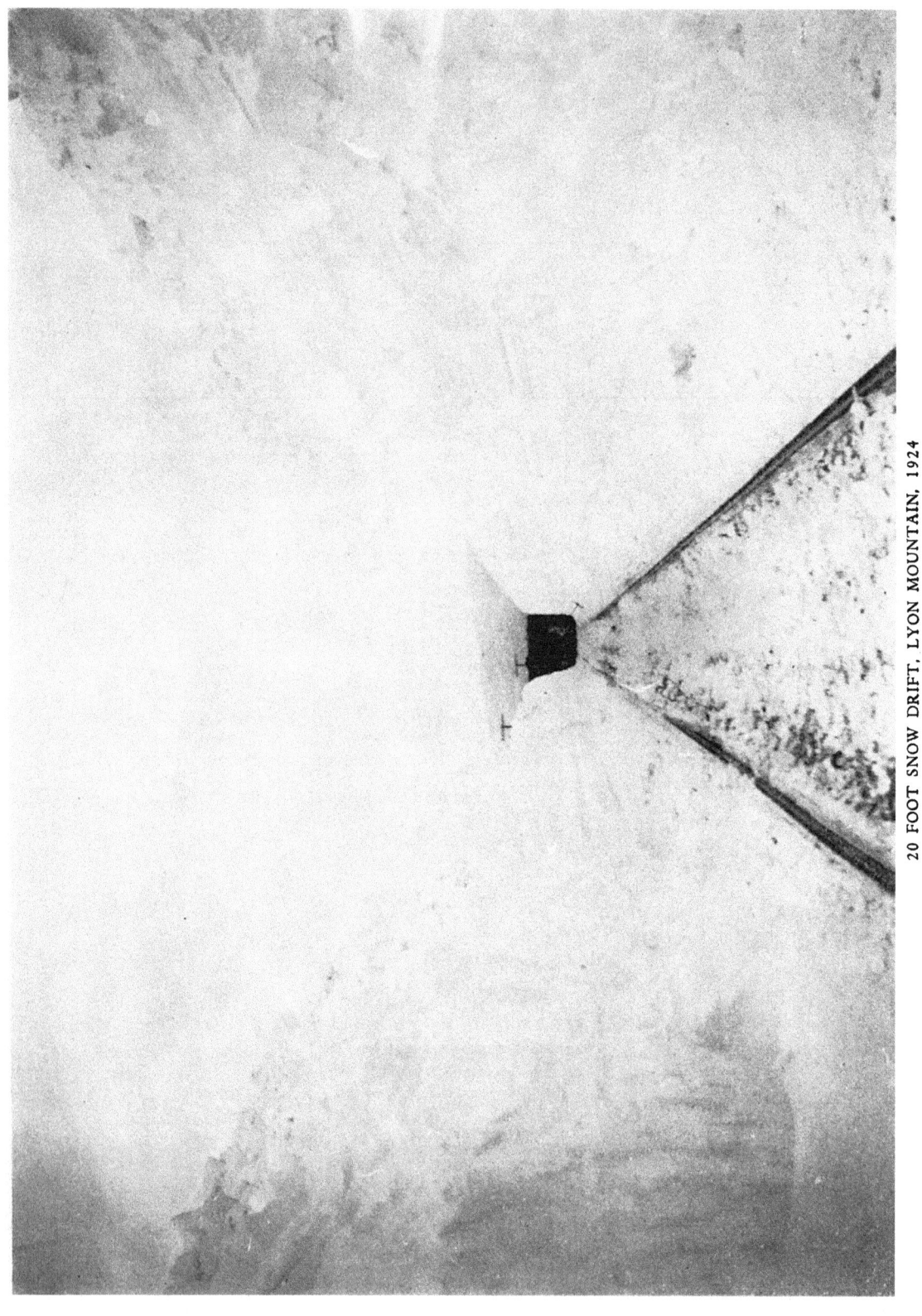

20 FOOT SNOW DRIFT, LYON MOUNTAIN, 1924

In 1921, it became necessary to make repairs and changes at the Standish Furnace, which included a new hearth and bosh, skip hoist and stock bins, pig casting machine, and a 25,000 cubic foot Turbo blower. In this connection, a sintering plant was built at Lyon Mountain, in order to sinter the concentrates for the furnace, and also to make additional sintered ore to be sold.

In May, 1924, the separator, which had been completed in 1918, was destroyed by fire. It had been intended to make this separator building entirely fireproof, but due to the difficulty in obtaining materials on account of the war, and the urgent need of the new separator because of the failure of the old No. 2 Separator, it had become necessary to use considerable wood in the construction of the interior of the building.

Plans were made, and work immediately started, on the building of a new and larger separator and concentrating plant, which was built entirely of steel and concrete, making it absolutely fireproof. This was completed and put in operation in June, 1925.

By the year 1925, the plants and equipment of the Company were modern in every way, including a well developed mine, with one main hoisting shaft, with steel headframe and concrete and steel hoist house; a large and modern concentrating plant, both built of steel and concrete, being absolutely fireproof; at the furnace, a skip hoist and bins, pig casting machine, turbo blower, a cooling system and a revolving distributor. The subsequent years have been devoted entirely to operating the plant and marketing the products.

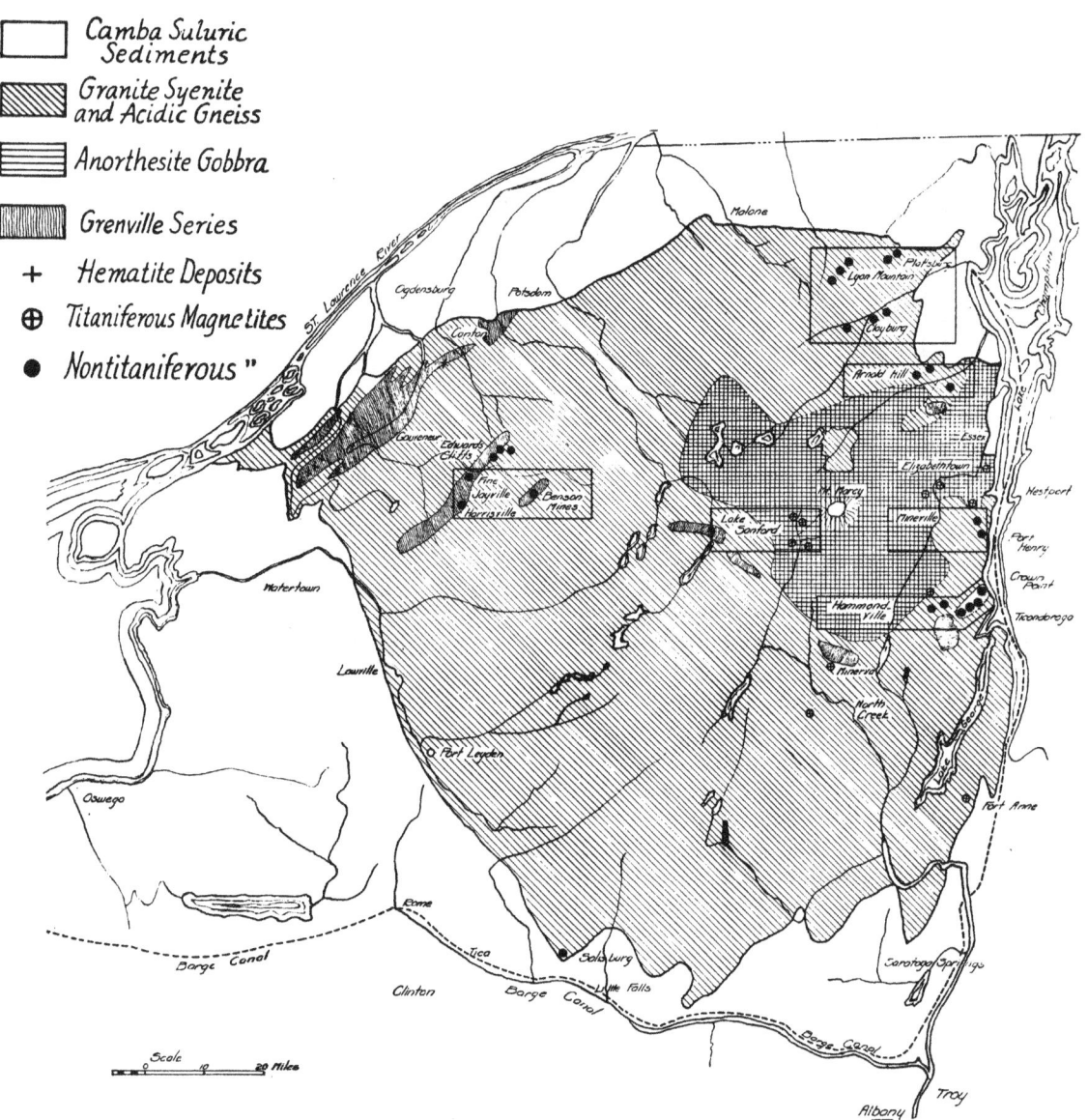

MAP SHOWING THE AREAL DISTRIBUTION OF THE PRINCIPAL ROCK FORMATIONS OF THE ADIRONDACKS AND OF THE IRON MINING AREAS (REPRODUCED FROM BULLETIN 119, NEW YORK STATE MUSEUM). AREA 1—LYON MOUNTAIN AND SARANAC. AREA 2—ARNOLD HILL. AREA 3—MINEVILLE-PORT HENRY. AREA 4—LAKE SANFORD. AREA 5—HAMMONDVILLE-CROWN POINT. AREA 6—BENSON MINES. AREAS ENCLOSED BEAR NO RELATION TO EXTENT OR VOLUME OF ORE DEPOSITS. BARGE CANAL, PLATTSBURG-BUFFALO, SHOWN BY DOTTED LINE.

Chapter III

GEOLOGY

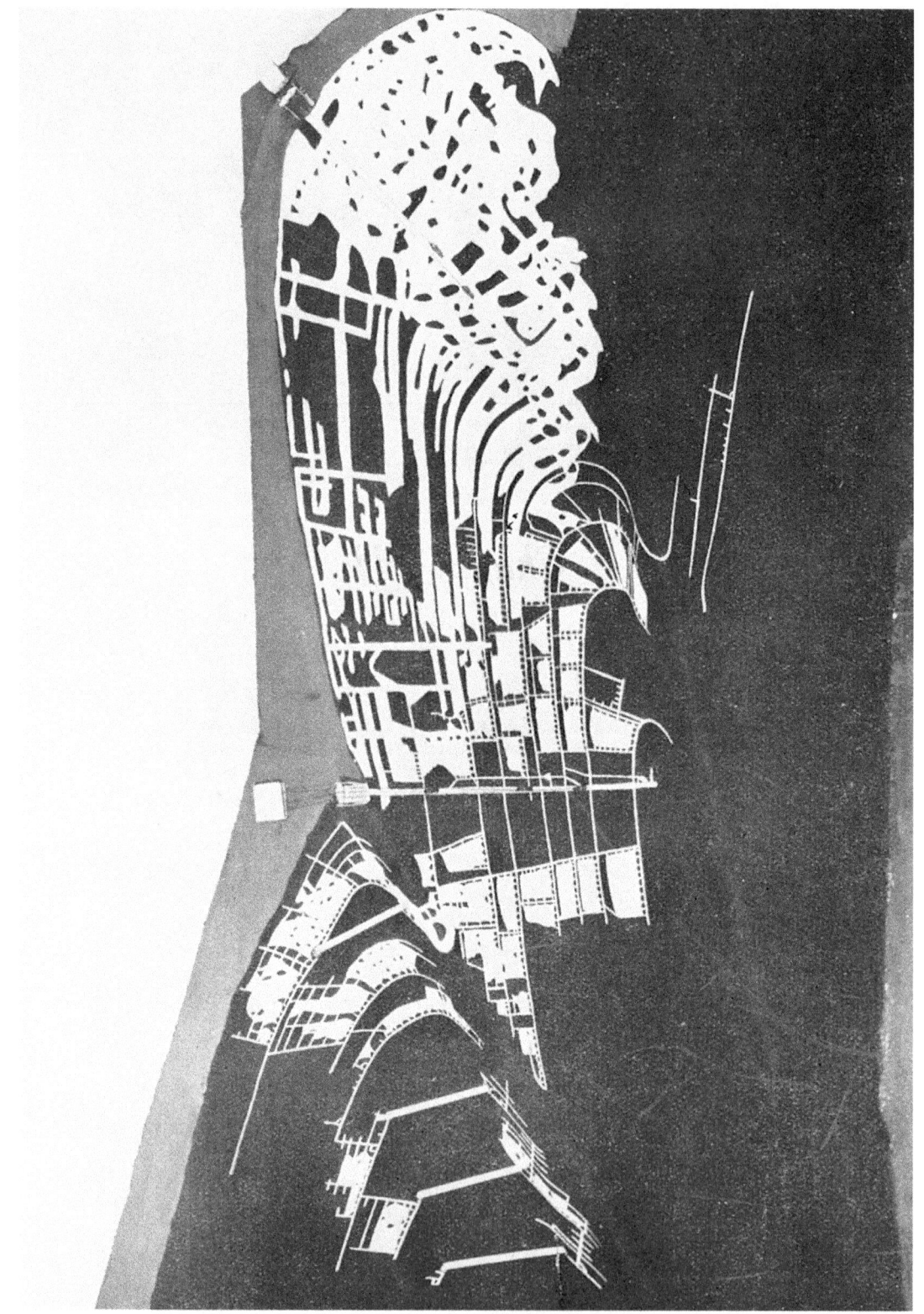

MODEL OF CHATEAUGAY MINE. WHITE INDICATES MINED AREA. BLACK INDICATES ORE INTACT

Geology

The Chateaugay iron ore, a magnetite, (Fe_3O_4,) practically free from phosphorus, sulphur, copper, chromium, arsenic and all other impurities, the purest and best iron ore to be found anywhere in the world, was formed in the Archaen period of the Archaeozoic era, and was, of course, Pre-Cambrian, and probably previous to any vegetable or animal life.

The formation is of igneous origin; eruptions of molten lava; in other words, volcanic. The rocks associated with the ore are all of the high temperature variety, (metamorphic) consisting chiefly of granitic gneiss, feldspar and hornblende. At some time subsequent to the formation, further disturbances occurred, which caused pronounced folding of the ore body and its associated rocks, and also the occasional intrusion of diabase trap rock dikes. These dikes, varying from a few inches to 20 feet in width, length unknown, usually cut across the ore body at right angles to the strike, displacing the ore, and very often faulting it.

The ore body consists of a series of folded lenses, varying in thickness from one foot to 120 feet, the general strike being northeast and southwest, dipping to the northwest, and pitching to the north. There are no well defined cleavage lines between the ore body and the foot and hanging walls. The width of the commercial ore is determined by drilling, sampling and assaying frequently, endeavoring to secure an average of 28% iron or better.

While there is a great and universal regularity in the general strike, dip and pitch of this ore body, and its associated rocks, many distortions and interruptions occur, such as the shifting of the vein, due to intrusive dikes and faults, the petering out of the ore lenses in places, often caused by intrusion of the country rock, and anticlinal folds.

When mining this ore body, it is of utmost economic importance that a complete knowledge be had of these interruptions and distortions and their effects, so that when they are encountered, the direction, in which to proceed to relocate the ore, may be determined with reasonable accuracy.

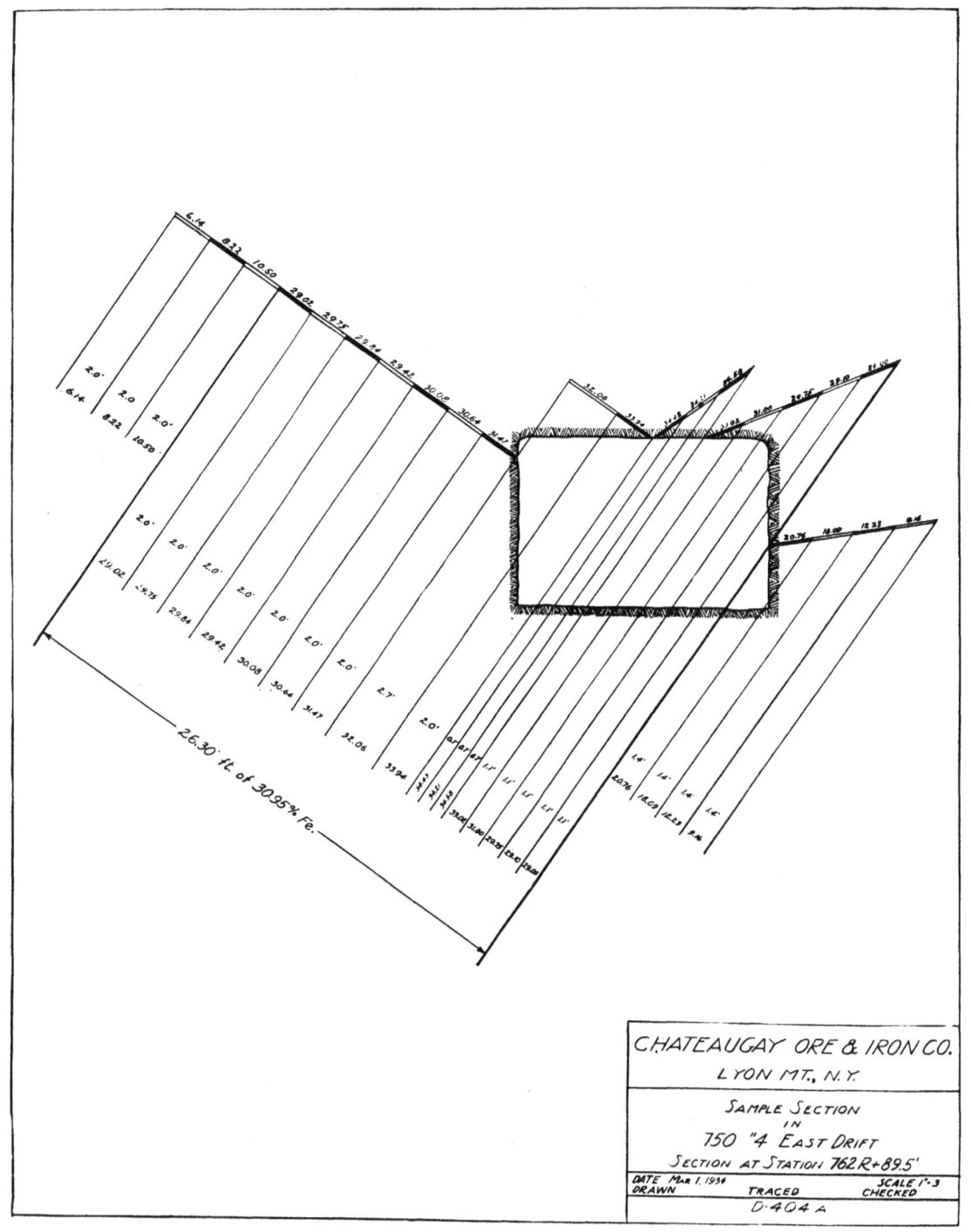

SAMPLE SECTION OF 750 FOOT LEVEL, NO. 4 EAST DRIFT

The results of the exploration work started by President Loree in 1907, and completed in 1914, showed that the Chateaugay Ore Bed contained commercial ore, 28 per cent iron, in quantities as follows:

Proven	15,000,000 long tons
Very probable	100,000,000 " "
Probable	200,000,000 " "
Possible	400,000,000 " "

The information made available by this exploration work has been invaluable as an aid in the development of the mine, and it has been proven to be amazingly accurate. After 15 years of extensive development, there are now 80,000,000 long tons proven and in sight.

The depth and extent to which the ore body continues east and west, along the strike, are still unknown, but information now available would indicate that the 400,000,000 tons, classed as "possible," in the geological estimate, might be classed as "very probable."

PRESENT HEADFRAME, HOIST HOUSE AND CHANGE HOUSE, NO. 1 SHAFT, CHATEAUGAY MINE

Chapter IV

MINING AND MANUFACTURING CHATEAUGAY PRODUCTS

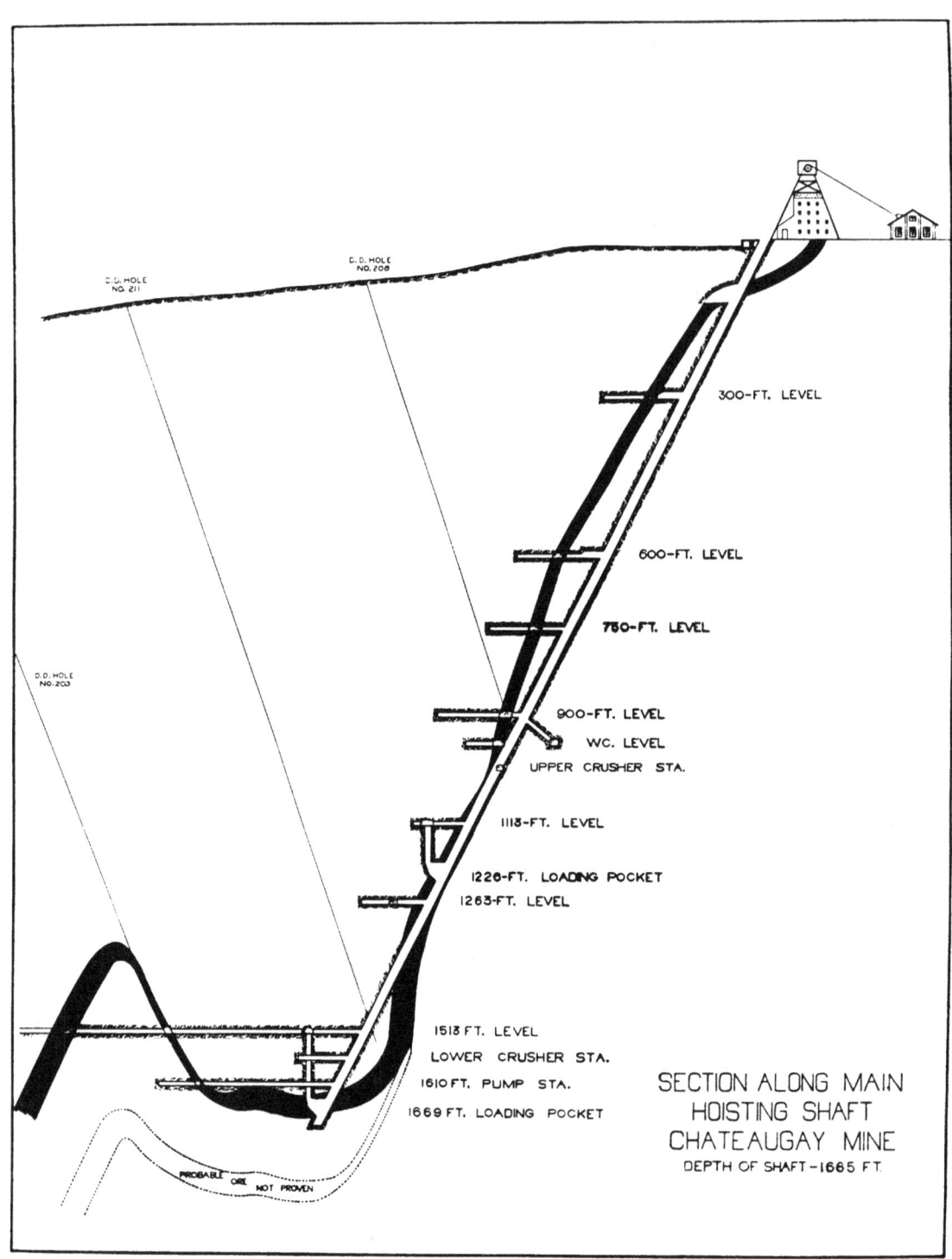

SECTION ALONG MAIN HOISTING SHAFT, CHATEAUGAY MINE

Mining and Manufacturing Chateaugay Products

Mining

The purpose of mining is to extract, economically, the minerals sought, by digging or burrowing in, or below, the surface of the earth.

The main entrance to the mine is through an 8 ft. x 24 ft., 63 degree incline shaft, sunk, mostly in the footwall, to a depth of 1,685 feet, the vein being tapped from the shaft at suitable intervals, varying from 150 to 300 feet.

Levels, or drifts, 8 ft. x 12 ft., are driven east and west of the shaft, on the strike of the vein. The drifts are driven on a rising grade of $\frac{3}{4}$ of 1 per cent in order to facilitate drainage and favor transportation, the loaded cars traveling on the down-grade. As the drifts advance, a permanent 36" gauge track is laid, with 40 lb. steel rail, on good, sound, wooden ties, spaced 30" apart, ballasted with iron ore, or rock, whichever the drift might be driven through.

Wherever the vein is steep enough, which it is in most places, raises 5 ft. x 8 ft., spaced on 30 foot centers, are driven up into the ore above the drift, from which stopes are started, for mining the ore for production. Chutes, usually made of 3 inch hardwood plank and timber, are installed in the bottom of the raises, through which the ore, after it has been broken, is loaded into the tram cars. At each end of a stope, a manway raise, 6 ft. x 8 ft., is driven through to the level above for ventilation, pipe and ladderways, and to afford entrance to the stopes.

There are three kinds of stoping methods used in winning the ore: shrinkage, underhand and scraper.

The shrinkage method consists of drilling up into the ore, blasting it down, and drawing only enough ore out of the stope each day to leave space for the men to work, completing a daily cycle, which is continued until the stope is advanced to within 30 feet of the level above, during which time about 40 per cent of the ore broken is drawn out daily, and 60 per cent left in. Thus, when the stope is completed, it is full of broken ore which can be drawn out at will.

DRIFTING ON VEIN, CHATEAUGAY MINE, 1933.

STOPING ORE, CHATEAUGAY MINE, 1933

ORE CHUTE, BOTTOM OF STOPE, CHATEAUGAY MINE

The underhand method consists of drilling down into the ore, and blasting it from sublevels which have been driven across the stope at 50 foot intervals, connecting both manway raises. As the ore is broken, it falls by gravity to the loading chutes below, and can all be drawn out immediately.

The scraper method is used in places where the vein is not steep enough for the ore to run by gravity. At convenient locations, a small, double drum, electrically driven hoist is installed, equipped with 5/8" steel cables, to which is attached a steel scraper. After the ore has been drilled and blasted, it is scraped along the floor to small ore pockets, from which it is loaded by gravity into the tram cars.

The drilling of the ore is done by high powered, compressed air drilling machines of various types and sizes, depending upon the character of work to be performed. Due to the extreme hardness and abrasiveness of the ore and rock, the drill steel used must be of the highest grade obtainable, and it is, therefore, made from Chateaugay iron.

Because of the hardness and density of the ore and rock, it is necessary to use high explosives in all cases for blasting.

Drill sharpening shops are located on each level for sharpening the drill steel, of which thousands of pieces are used and dulled daily. The drillers, including those on development work, average 31 long tons drilled and blasted per man per 8-hour day.

The transportation of the ore from the working places to the main hoisting shaft is accomplished by electric, storage battery locomotives, and steel, Granby type, side dump cars, each having a capacity of six long tons, and equipped with roller bearings. The loading and tramming of each train is done by two men, averaging 55 long tons per man per day for the entire mine.

After the ore is trammed to the main hoisting shaft, it is dumped into the ore pass which is connected to each level, and at the bottom of which is located a large 48" x 36" Jaw crusher for crushing the lumps of ore down to 8 inches and smaller. The material from the crusher is discharged by gravity into the skip loading bins, where it is loaded into the 8-ton skips, hoisted at the rate of 1,800 feet per minute, and dumped automatically into the bins above the secondary crushers in the headframe at the top of the shaft.

The mine is splendidly ventilated in a rather unique and inexpensive way. The openings from the old workings to the surface at the extreme westerly end of the mine are considerably higher than those on the easterly end. During the long, cold winter months, tremendous quantities of ice, hundreds of thousands of tons, accumulate in these workings, which cools the air sufficiently to cause large volumes to go down into the workings, forcing the smoke and gases out through the openings to the surface on the easterly end of the mine. The ice, of course, melts considerably during the summer months, but never

DRILL SHARPENING SHOP, PRESENT CHATEAUGAY MINE

STORAGE BATTERY LOCOMOTIVE AND ORE TRAIN, CHATEAUGAY MINE, 1933

ELECTRIC HOIST, NO. 1 SHAFT, PRESENT CHATEAUGAY MINE

entirely, enough fortunately remaining to insure ample ventilation of the mine at all times.

The entire mine is so arranged that the water from all sections drains by gravity to points at, or near, the main hoisting shaft, from which it is pumped to the surface by electrically driven pumps. The quantity of water amounts to about 500 gallons per minute. It is very pure, contains no acids, and is therefore not destructive to the pumping equipment.

In many places in the mine, especially on the lower levels, a great deal of timbering must be done in order to support the back, or roof, of the main drifts, on account of the tendency of the ore and rock to spall and loosen.

The mine, as developed and equipped at the present time, is capable of producing 2,000 long tons of ore per 8-hour day, averaging 15 long tons per man per 8-hour day for all underground workmen.

Milling and Concentrating

The purpose of milling and concentrating is to beneficiate the iron ore by separating and eliminating from it, insofar as is economically possible, all of the rock and other materials that might be associated with it when it comes from the mine. The Chateaugay ore, as mined, contains 28 per cent iron. By milling and concentrating, the iron content is brought up to 69 per cent. Pure magnetite contains 72.4 per cent iron and 27.6 per cent oxygen.

When the ore comes from the mine, it is 8" and smaller in size. The fines, 2½" and smaller, are screened out by a rotary grizzly, and the larger pieces crushed to 2½" and smaller, by two 10" x 72" jaw crushers in the headhouse, at the top of the main hoisting shaft. The ore is then conveyed, at the rate of 250 tons per hour, by a 30" belt conveyor, to two 750 ton storage bins; from the bottom of which it is conveyed, at the rate of 250 tons per hour, by a 30" belt conveyor to the primary roll house, the first unit of the concentrating plant.

The ore is now passed over vibrating screens with one inch square openings. The portion which passes over the screens goes to two 36" pulley type, electro-magnetic separators which are set and regulated to discard all material containing less than 6 per cent iron. This material is known as "coarse tailings," and is sent to the tailings pile. The iron bearing material retained by the separators is discharged, by gravity, to a set of 20" x 72", plain faced, chrome steel rolls, and is ground to 1½" and smaller.

The material that passes through the screens, and which contains about 4 per cent moisture, by weight, discharges by gravity into a 150 ton bin, from which it is elevated about 100 feet, vertically, by a belt and bucket type elevator, and discharged into the dryer. The dryer is a steel stack, about 125 feet high,

LARGE QUINTIPLEX PUMP IN PRESENT CHATEAUGAY MINE

HEAVY TIMBER ON MAIN DRIFT, LOWER LEVELS, CHATEAUGAY MINE, 1933

MAIN HAULAGE WAY, SHOWING TIMBERED SECTION, CHATEAUGAY MINE

lined with fire brick, and equipped with cast iron baffles, the purpose of which is to retard the ore, as it falls down through the stack. Hot gases, by which the ore is dried, are produced by a Coxe stoker, burning birdseye anthracite and located near the bottom of the dryer stack.

The material as it comes from the dryer, thoroughly dry, is conveyed by a 24" steel conveyor and discharged, along with the material from the rolls, onto a 30" belt conveyor, and sent direct to the secondary roll house, the second unit of the concentrating plant.

The material is now passed over double deck vibrating screens, having 10 mesh openings on the bottom deck. The portion that passes over the screens goes to four 36", pulley type, electro-magnetic separators, which are set and regulated to discard all material containing less than 6 per cent iron. This material is known as medium size ore tailings, and is sent to the tailings pile. The material retained by the separators is discharged by gravity to three sets of 24" x 54", plain faced, chrome steel rolls. The material, after leaving the rolls, is returned, in closed circuit, to the screens at the top of the building.

The material that passes through the screens is sent to a 30 foot, centrifugal air separator for taking out all of the minus 100 mesh material, which is sent direct to the wet magnetic separators, in the concentrator house, the third and last unit of the concentrating plant. The coarse material from the air separator, which is minus 10 mesh, and plus 100 mesh, is conveyed, by a 30" belt conveyor, direct to the bins over the dry, magnetic separators, in the concentrator house.

The minus 10 mesh, dry material now passes over 16–30", drum type, electro-magnetic separators, making a concentrate containing 69 per cent iron and better, and a tailing containing not more than 3 per cent iron. The middlings from these separators fall by gravity to 16 similar type separators directly below, which also make a concentrate containing 69 per cent iron and better, and a tailing containing not more than 3 per cent iron. The middlings from these separators are returned to the bins at the top of the building in closed circuit. The concentrates are sent to two 500-ton storage bins, at the top of the sintering plant, and the tailings are sent to the tailings pile.

Because the minus 100 mesh material cannot be efficiently separated on dry drum type magnetic separators, it is sent to 8 belt type wet magnetic separators where, as it passes over the magnetic field, the tailings or gangue is thoroughly washed out by a spray of water. These separators make a 70 per cent iron concentrate, and a tailing containing not more than 2 per cent iron. The concentrates are sent to the storage bins above the sintering plant.

The ore tailings, or rock that has been separated from the ore, has become a very valuable by-product during the last ten years. Each commercial size is stored separately in piles above a concrete tunnel, through which a 36" belt conveyor takes it to railroad cars for shipment to market.

PRESENT CHATEAUGAY CONCENTRATING PLANT, LYON MOUNTAIN

PRESENT CONTROL ROOM, CONCENTRATING PLANT, LYON MOUNTAIN

PULLEY TYPE MAGNETIC SEPARATORS FOR COBBING ROCK OUT OF THE ORE

The concentrating plant has a capacity for treating, efficiently, 2,000 long tons of ore in 8 hours as it comes from the mine, from which 800 long tons of concentrates, containing 69 per cent iron, are produced.

Sintering

The purpose of sintering is to improve the physical character of the concentrated ore by fusing the ore particles into a cellular mass, which makes it much more desirable for use in the blast furnaces, where most of it goes.

Sintering is accomplished, at this plant, by means of a Dwight & Lloyd, continuous machine, 6 ft. wide and 69 ft. long, comprised of a series of perforated grates, known as pallets, which are mounted on wheels for traveling on a continuous track.

The concentrated ore is first mixed with about $5\frac{1}{2}$ per cent by weight of anthracite. The fuel is about the size of granulated sugar, very high in carbon, and low in ash, and is known as Anthrafine. It is produced by the Hudson Coal Company, and is most desirable as a fuel for sintering purposes.

As the fuel and the concentrated ore are being mixed, by means of a pug mill, a small amount of water is added as a temporary binder. This mixture of ore and fuel is spread evenly on the pallets of the sintering machine, to a thickness of about 6 inches, and the fuel is immediately ignited as it passes under an oil heated ignition furnace, comprised of high temperature, refractory brick, and a retort, or combustion chamber, suspended by a steel and cast iron frame.

Combustion is assisted by a downward current of air, drawn through the mixture, or bed, the entire length of the machine, by a large induced draft fan.

The speed at which the machine travels is regulated so that, by the time the material reaches the discharge end, the fuel is entirely burned out and the process completed. The sinter is then discharged over a set of stationary grizzly bars, spaced one inch apart, which take out the fines, allowing only the coarse material to go to the railroad car for shipment. The fines are returned, by means of an inclined belt conveyor, and are mixed with the incoming feed to the sintering machine.

The plant has an output capacity of 50 long tons of sintered ore per hour, and can be opearted, continuously and efficiently, 16 hours daily, (two 8-hour shifts) or 24 hours daily, (three 8-hour shifts,) by suspending operations one day each week for maintenance and repairs.

A BATTERY OF VIBRATING SCREENS, PRESENT CHATEAUGAY CONCENTRATING PLANT

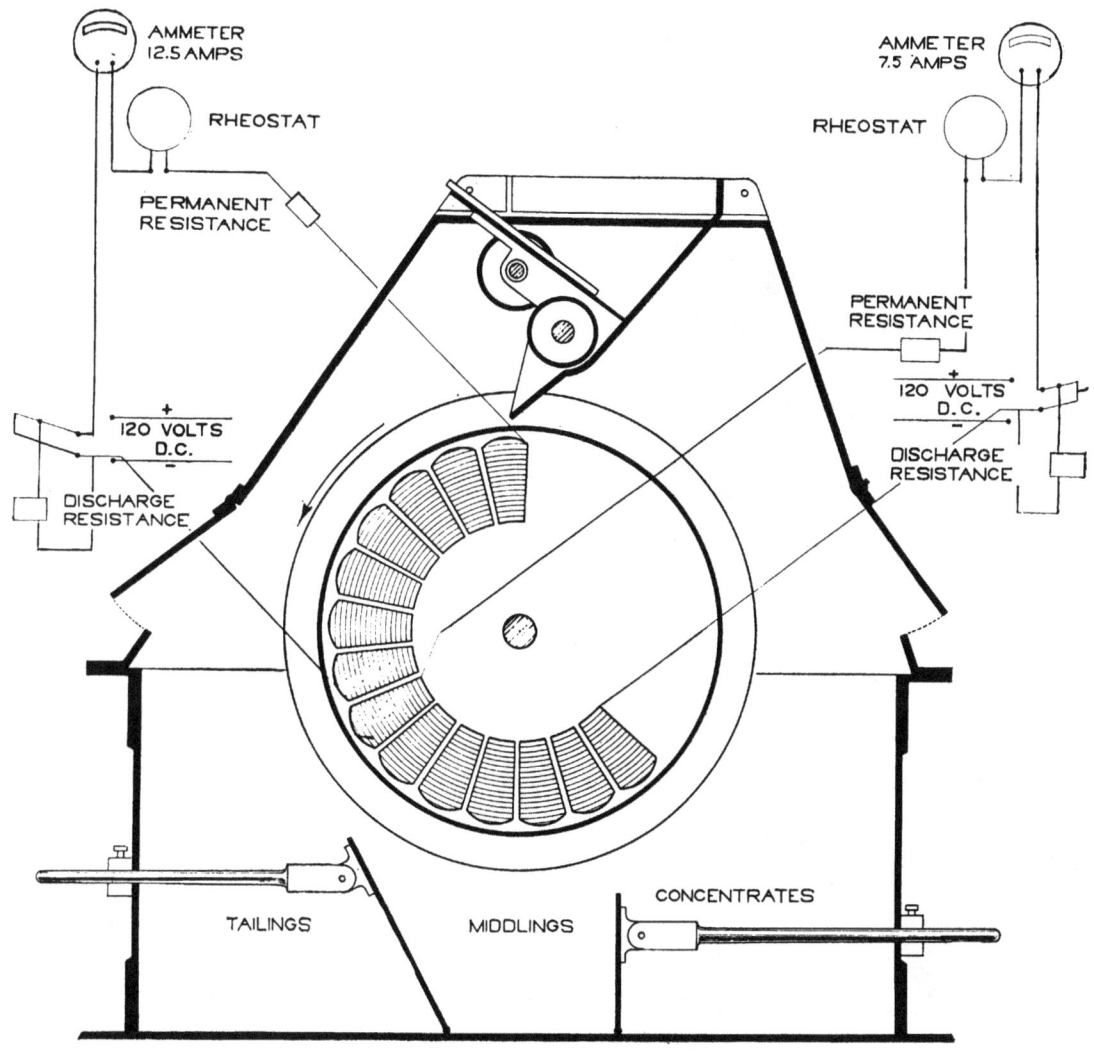

**LATEST IMPROVED TYPE
DRUM MAGNETIC SEPARATOR
USED IN CHATEAUGAY CONCENTRATING PLANT**

MAGNETIC SEPARATORS, PRESENT CHATEAUGAY CONCENTRATING PLANT

The Blast Furnace

The purpose for which the Blast Furnace is used is to reduce, or deoxidize, and smelt the iron ore (iron oxide), converting it from an oxide to a metallic state.

While the art of smelting iron ores in a blast furnace has been known for centuries, very little was generally understood of the phenomena until about the middle of the Nineteenth Century, when Sir Lowthian Bell published his first treatise in England on the chemical actions, and reactions, that take place inside the blast furnace. Much has since been learned, but Bell's fundamental principles continue undisputed. Bell, a learned metallurgist and chemist, amidst a very busy and active life, found time to determine, by reasoning and calculating, these phenomena.

The process of smelting iron in the blast furnace consists essentially of charging a mixture of fuel, ore and flux into the top of the furnace, and simultaneously blowing in a current of heated atmospheric air at the bottom. The air burns the fuel, forming heat for the chemical reactions and for melting the products; the gases formed by this combustion remove the oxygen from the ore, thereby reducing it to metallic form; the flux renders fluid the earthy materials. The gaseous products of the operation pass out at the top of the furnace, while the liquid products, cast iron and slag, are tapped at the bottom. The escaping gases are combustible, and therefore are conducted through pipes to boilers and stoves where they perform the useful services of heating the blast and generating steam for operating the engines.

It is evident, therefore, that several factors enter into the composition of a complete smelting unit. The central feature is the furnace with its hoists and skips for the handling of charges, and its ladles and pig machines for handling the products. Quite as essential are the blowing engines which drive the blast to the furnace, through a series of hot blast stoves, which heat the blast on its way. Not less important are the boiler plants and the pumps which furnish the power to drive the blowing engines and supply the vast quantities of water needed for cooling purposes.

The furnace proper is a large steel stack, about 80 feet high, lined inside with high temperature, refractory brick. It is comprised of three distinct parts, each having a different function. The shaft, or upper part of the furnace, has an inside diameter of 13 feet at the top, gradually increasing to 17 feet where it connects to the bosh, about two-thirds of the way down. The bosh, having an inside diameter of 17 feet at the top, where it connects to the bottom of the shaft, gradually decreases to a diameter of 13 feet at its bottom, where it connects to the top of the hearth. The hearth has a diameter of 13 feet straight down to its bottom, which is the bottom of the furnace.

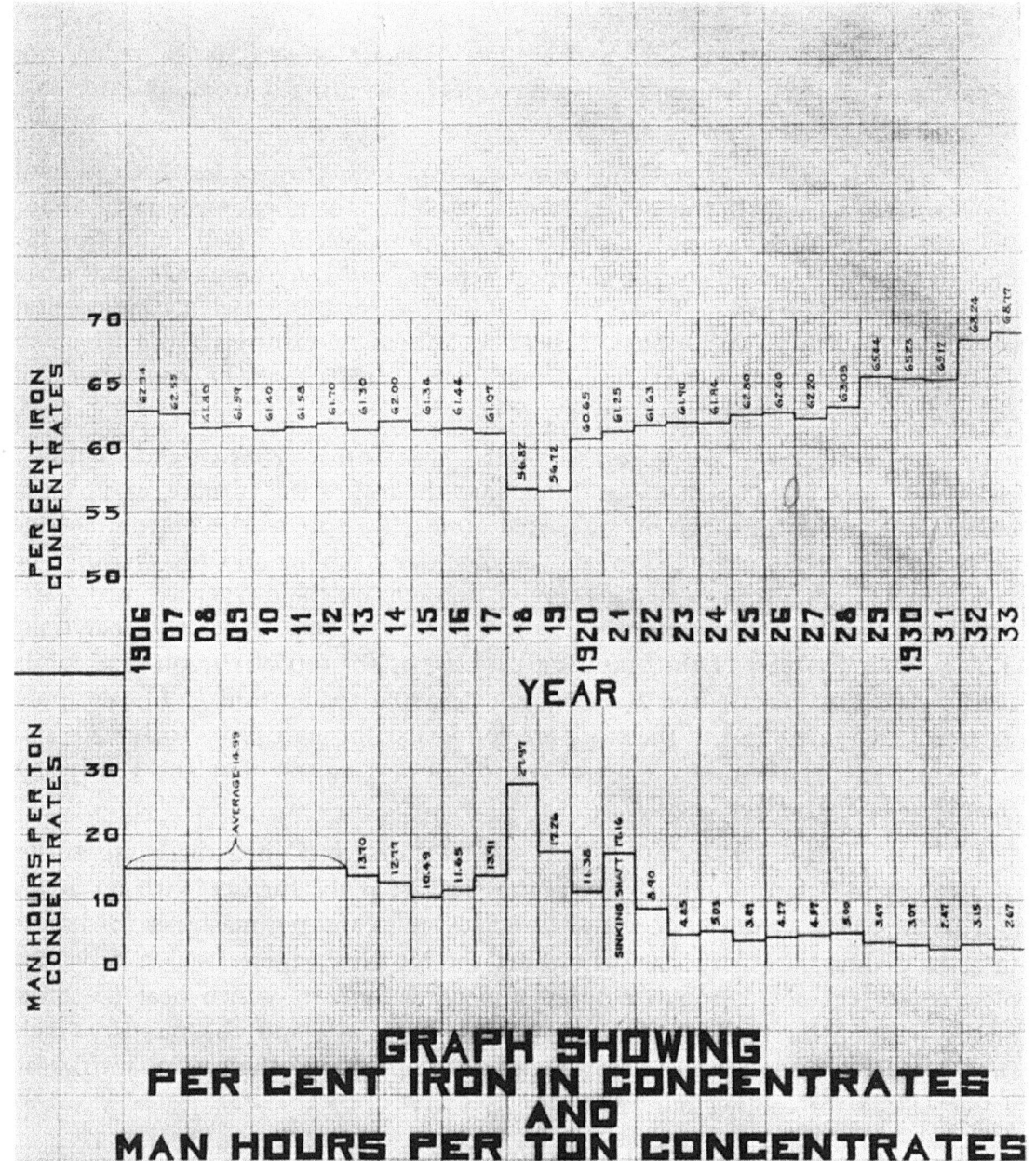

PRESENT CHATEAUGAY SINTERING PLANT, LYON MOUNTAIN

INTERIOR VIEW OF PRESENT CHATEAUGAY SINTERING PLANT

In order to protect and prolong the life of the brick lining, hollow bronze cooling plates are inserted at intervals, through which water is continually circulated.

The ratio of ore, and its accompanying flux, to the fuel of a furnace charge, is generally termed the "burden" of the furnace. The task of determining the quantity of each, which is best suited to furnace conditions, is designated as "burdening the furnace." The successful running of the furnace probably depends more upon burdening than upon any other single factor in its management. In the early days of the industry, before the constant application of chemical analysis to the materials used, burdening was a combination of previous experience and guesswork. If any raw materials from an unfamiliar source had to be used, the treatment required had to be guessed, until it could be determined by experience. With the application of analytical methods, however, it became possible to predict, with tolerable accuracy, the requirements of any materials from their chemical composition.

The raw materials are put into the furnace in alternate layers of coke, and a mixture of iron ore, limestone, and sometimes manganese bearing material. These are called "charges," and take up a space in the furnace from four feet to six feet in depth. The furnace is kept full, to within a few feet of the top, at all times.

The blast of air, which has been preheated to about 1,400 degrees Fahrenheit by the stoves, is forced into the furnace through pipes, connected to short, hollow, bronze, water cooled tubes, called "tuyeres," having an inside diameter of about 5 inches There are eight of these "tuyeres" evenly spaced around the upper part of the hearth, and just below the bottom of the bosh.

The carbon, liberated by the burning of the coke at the bottom of the furnace, unites with the oxygen of the incoming blast of air, forming large quantities of gaseous compounds, including carbon monoxide (CO). This gas has a great affinity for oxygen. Therefore, as it passes up through the raw materials in the shaft of the furnace, it unites with the oxygen in the iron ore, reducing the ore to a metallic state, and passes out through the top of the furnace as carbon dioxide (CO_2). There is always more than enough carbon monoxide present to completely reduce the iron ore. The remainder is burned under the boilers to make steam and in the stoves to preheat the blast of air

By the time the materials reach the top of the bosh, the iron ore is all reduced to a metallic state, and the carbon dioxide (CO_2) has been driven out of the limestone, changing it to lime ($CAO.$). The iron and slag forming materials begin to melt at this point, and trickle in streams down through the voids of the coke bed into the hearth. The molten iron, being heavier, goes to the bottom, and the molten slag, being lighter, rests on top of the iron. The slag is drawn from the furnace through the cinder notch at various intervals.

CHATEAUGAY SINTERED ORE AS IT GOES TO R. R. CARS

STANDISH FURNACE, 1933

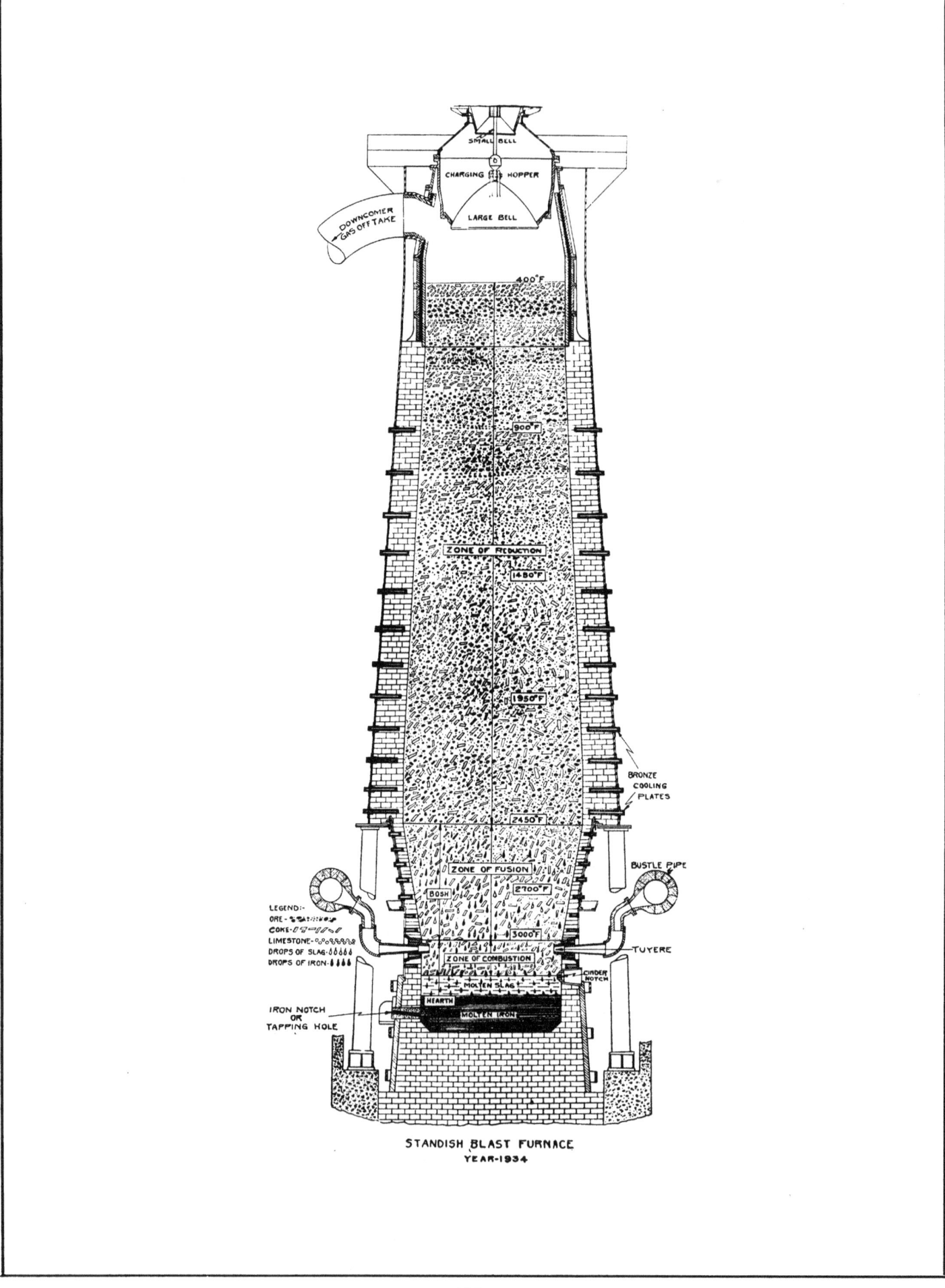

This is called "flushing." The iron is drawn from the furnace through the iron notch, periodically, from four to six times in 24 hours. This is called "casting."

The slag drawn from the furnace goes to large, standard gauge, ladle cars, and is sent directly to the slag dump. The quantity of iron drawn from the furnace, at cast time, will vary from 35 tons to 60 tons, depending upon how fast the furnace is driven, and it goes directly to a large 70-ton capacity ladle, which is lined with high temperature refractory brick.

At the end of the cast, the tapping hole, or iron notch, is plugged with fire clay, by means of a steam operated cylinder, known as the "mud-gun," and the blast again put on the furnace. Immediately after this has been done, the molten iron is poured from the ladle into the pig casting machine, a continuous strand of cast iron moulds, mounted on wheels and traveling on an inclined track. It is sprayed with a thin stream of hot water and steam, so that by the time it reaches the discharge end of the machine, is is solidified into small blocks of iron, weighing about 65 pounds each, called "pigs." It is then discharged directly into the railroad car, from where it is sent either to the storage yard or to market.

The ingredients from which Chateaugay iron is made are coke, limestone, Chateaugay sintered ore and, when making manganese bearing iron, manganese residuum, a product from ferro-manganese furnaces, is added. All of these materials contain certain elements that must be eliminated from the iron in the process of manufacture. It is, therefore, necessary to know the exact chemical composition of each ingredient before it is put into the furnace. This is learned by sampling and analyzing the materials daily. When any appreciable change in chemical composition of any of the materials is discovered, the burden must be changed accordingly.

The principal detrimental elements that high grade pig iron should be kept free of are sulphur, phosphorus, chromium, copper and arsenic. The Chateaugay iron is entirely free from chromium, copper and arsenic, because none of the raw materials used in its manufacture contain any of these elements. Sulphur enters the furnace in the coke, and is nearly all eliminated in the slag. Phosphorus enters the furnace in slight amounts in the ore and in the coke. It has a greater affinity for molten iron than for the slag and, therefore, all of the phosphorus that goes into the furnace enters the iron. The Chateaugay iron is very low in phosphorus, because the ore from which it is made is practically free from that element. This is also true of the coke and limestone used.

There are at least 35 different and distinct varieties of Chateaugay iron made and sold to the trade. All of these grades are amazingly free from impurities, and are distinguished by the percentages of different metalloids contained therein, such as silicon, carbon and manganese.

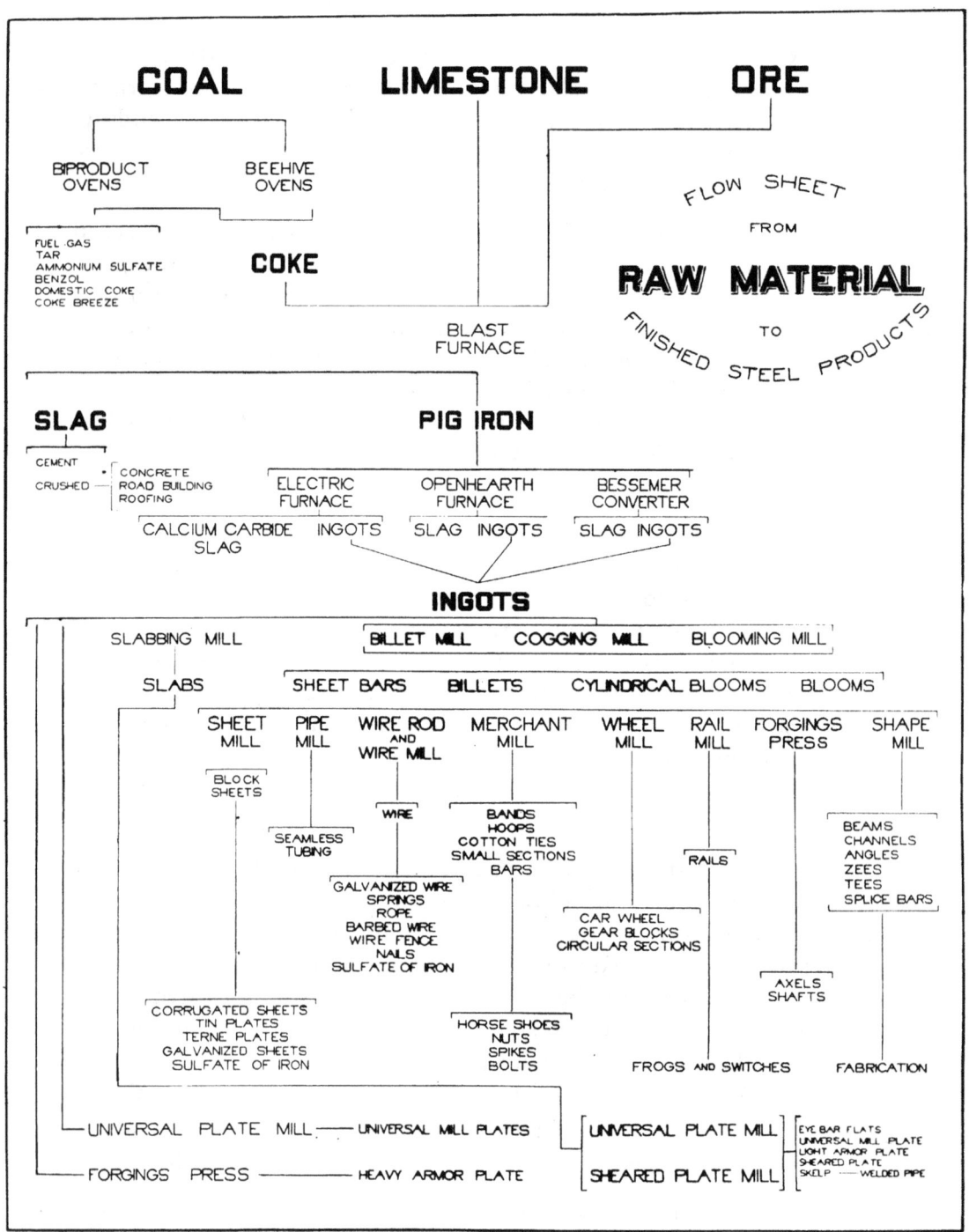

FLOW SHEET FROM RAW MATERIALS TO FINISHED PRODUCTS

CASTING MOLTEN IRON, STANDISH FURNACES, 1933

PRESENT STANDISH BLAST FURNACE

When making the various kinds of iron, the furnaceman has at his command three variables, by which he must achieve the desired results. They are the heat, burden composition and slag composition. With sufficient heat, properly composed burdens and properly composed slags, a wide range of products may be obtained from identical materials. The proper amount of heat in the furnace is that which will maintain the least temperature necessary to perform the work desired; any excess is waste. The temperature which is necessary to obtain given results depends upon the product desired, and is inseparably linked with the slag composition. Generally speaking, the slag is the substance that requires the highest temperature for its proper function and disposal and, when that temperature has been attained, it is ample for all other purposes.

The slag serves a two fold purpose in the furnace. It is the means by which the temperature of the hearth is controlled, and also by which the sulphur is kept out of the iron. If it is too fluid, it will flow down through the voids of the coke bed rapidly, without absorbing and carrying sufficient heat down into the hearth. If it is too viscous, it will not flow through the voids, but will clog up the furnace, prevent the free passage of the upward flow of the gases and interfere with the regular movement of the stock in the furnace, making it necessary to check, or take the blast off entirely, at frequent intervals until the condition has been corrected.

It will, therefore, be readily seen that it is highly important to arrange for the composition of a slag that will not be too fluid nor too viscous, but will have a consistency which will allow it to flow freely and slowly through the voids of the coke bed, in order to function properly.

In addition to the above, it is highly important that the chemical composition of the slag be such that it will have a greater attraction for the sulphur than the iron, the slag being the only positive means of eliminating the sulphur, practically all of which enters the blast furnace in the coke. Under favorable conditions, the sulphur will unite with the lime in the slag, forming calcium sulphide. If conditions are unfavorable, it will unite with the iron, forming ferrous-sulphide and spoiling the iron.

As previously stated, the phosphorus content of the pig iron is practically independent of furnace manipulation, but depends almost entirely upon the nature of the materials used. Probably never less than 90 per cent of the phosphorus present enters the iron, and more often it is nearer 100 per cent. Therefore, in order that this element be kept out of the iron, it must not enter the furnace.

The quantity of carbon which enters the pig iron is independent of the furnace burden. It is present in two forms: graphitic and combined. The sum of the two is known as "Total Carbon," which ranges from 3.00% to 4.50% in the pig iron. Carbon comes from the coke, and is deposited in the

CHATEAUGAY ORE AND IRON COMPANY
BURDEN SHEET - STANDISH BLAST FURNACE

STOCK ANALYSIS IN PER CENT

STOCK	FE	SiO2	Al2O3	CaO	MgO	P	MN	S
Ore	69.00	2.50	1.06	.30	.24	.003	.10	-
Tailings	6.00	54.50	10.92	6.90	3.14	.062	-	-
Sand								
Mang. Res.								
Coke	.62	5.40	3.17	.18	.022	.009	-	.82
Limestone	-	1.46	.86	53.86	.65	-	-	-

WEIGHT OF CHARGE IN POUNDS

STOCK	POUNDS	FE	SiO2	Al2O3	CaO	MgO	P	MN	S
Ore	11000	7590	275	117	33	26	.33	11.00	-
Tailings	1000	60	545	109	69	31	.62	-	-
Sand									
Mang.Res.									
Coke	6400	40	346	203	12	1	.58	-	52.48
TOTAL		7690	1166	429	114	58	1.53	11.00	52.48
Reqd. for Iron			263						
NET TOTAL			903	429	114	58	1.53	11.00	52.48
Limestone	2100		30	18	1131	14			
Slag Composition			933	447	1245	72		5.00	42.97

7690 Lbs Fe ÷ .94 Fe in Iron = 8181 Lbs Yield ÷ 2240 = 3.65 Tons Yield.

SiO2 for Iron = 8181 Lbs Yield x 1.50% Si in Iron x 2.14 = 263 Lbs.

MnO in Slag = 1/3 x 11.00 x 1.29 = 5 Lbs.

S in Iron = .02 x 8181 =	1.64 Lbs	Net Total SiO2 in charge =	903 Lbs.
S Volatilized = .15 x 52.48 =	7.87 Lbs	Less (114 + 58) ÷ 1.4	= 123 Lbs
Total	9.51 Lbs	Net SiO2 to Flux	= 780 Lbs
Total S in charge =	52.48 Lbs	780 x 2.67 = 2083 Lbs. Limestone Reqd.	
Less	9.51 Lbs		
Net Lbs. S. to Flux	42.97 Lbs		

SILICON FOR IRON	LIME-SILICA RATIO	STONE FACTOR
Under 1.00%	1.5 to 1	2.87
1.00 to 1.60%	1.4 to 1	2.67
1.75 and Over	1.3 to 1	2.47

	SLAG PRODUCED		IRON PRODUCED	
	POUNDS	PER CENT		PER CENT
SiO2	933	33.99	Fe	94.00
Al2O3	447	16.28	Si	1.50
CaO	1245	45.36	S	.02
MgO	72	2.62	P	.019
MnO	5	.18	Mn	.073
S	43	1.57		
Total	2745	100.00		

1245 + 72 ÷ 933 = 1.41

Lime Silica Ratio Desired - 1.4 to 1	Pounds Slag per ton iron - 752
Average Iron Content of Burden - 63.75	Pounds Slag per ton coke - 858
Burden Ratio - 1.88 to 1	Pounds coke per ton iron - 1753

TYPICAL BURDEN AIMING AT 1.50 SILICON IRON WITHOUT MANGANESE

iron in various amounts, depending upon the temperature of the hearth and the other metalloids in the iron.

Silicon in the iron varies from 0.50% to 4.50%, depending almost entirely upon the manipulation of the furnace. It is produced by reducing, or deoxidizing, the silica under high temperature. It has a very strong affinity for molten iron. Due to its importance, it is the one element, more than any other, that is responsible for the grading of the iron into so many varieties.

Manganese in the iron varies in percentages from 0.00% to 2.50%. It has little or no effect in amounts under 0.15%. Chateaugay iron is made with or without manganese. About 75% of the total manganese that enters the furnace goes into the iron. Some of it goes out with the slag as an oxide, and the remainder is lost by volatilization.

The Chateaugay iron is made entirely from Chateaugay ore. No foreign scrap of any kind is put into the furnace. In other words, it is an all-ore pig iron and, without a doubt, the purest to be found anywhere.

In connection with the blast furnace, there is a small iron foundry, used for making iron castings. The molten metal used comes directly from the blast furnace and is run into small ladles for pouring the castings.

The pig iron, after it is made into pigs, is all carefully weighed, and either goes directly to market or to the storage yard, where it is piled separately according to its chemical composition. When iron is taken out of storage for shipment to market, the railroad car is first thoroughly cleaned, and weighed light, and is again carefully weighed after it is loaded.

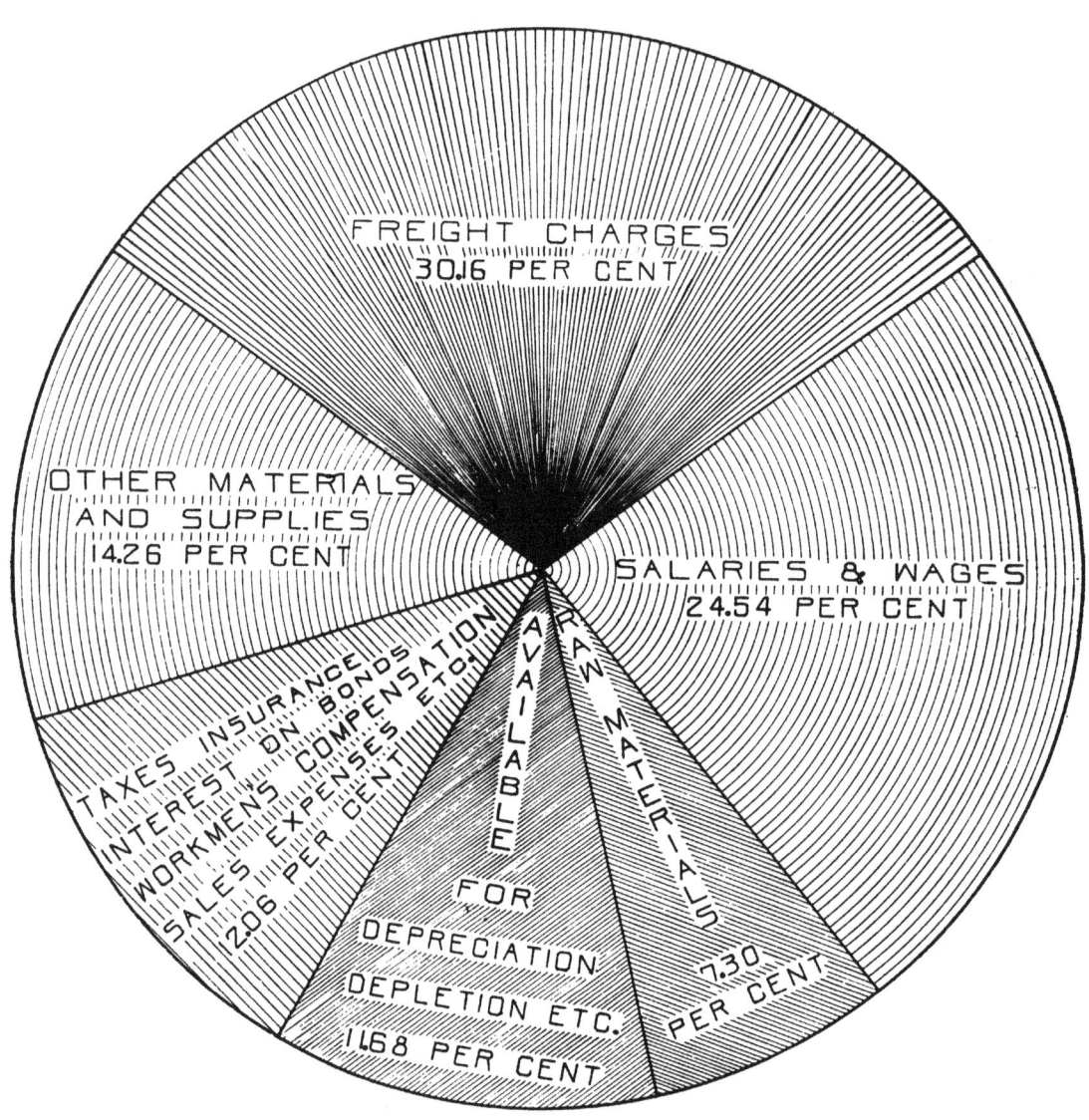

PER CENT ITEMS OF COSTS
CHATEAUGAY PIG IRON

Chapter V

SALES AND DISTRIBUTION OF CHATEAUGAY PRODUCTS

AWARD FOR QUALITY, WORLD'S FAIR 1893

Sales and Distribution of Chateaugay Products

The Company produces and sells the following products:
Low phosphorus, copper free, run of mine magnetic iron ore.
Low phosphorus, copper free, concentrated magnetic iron ore.
Low phosphorus, copper free, sintered magnetic iron ore.
Low phosphorus, copper free, pig iron.
Iron castings.
Iron ore tailings, sand and stone sizes (by-product).
Pulpwood, hardwood, and other varieties of timber (products of woodlands).

There has not been very much demand for run of mine ore, but developments are underway and preparations are being made to produce and prepare material suitable for use in the open hearth steel furnaces, and it is expected that it will be in great demand.

The concentrated ore will pass through a 10 mesh screen. It is a highly refined product. Its approximate chemical analysis is as follows:

Iron	69.00 per cent.
Silica	2.50 " "
Alumina	1.00 " "
Lime	.36 " "
Magnesium	.34 " "
Phosphorus	.002 " "
Manganese	.07 " "
Sulphur	Trace.
Chromium	Free.
Copper	Free.
Arsenic	Free.

(Note: The difference between the above total and 100% is oxygen).

Concentrated ore is very desirable for the following uses: making pure sponge iron by the direct process; in the electric furnace; in the puddling furnace; beneficiating flue dust for sintering; and mixing with, or sweetening, high phosphorus ores.

The sintered ore is a cellular, lumpy product, highly refined, and has the same chemical analysis as the concentrated ore. It has no equal as a blast furnace product. It is sold in large quantities to blast furnace companies, for

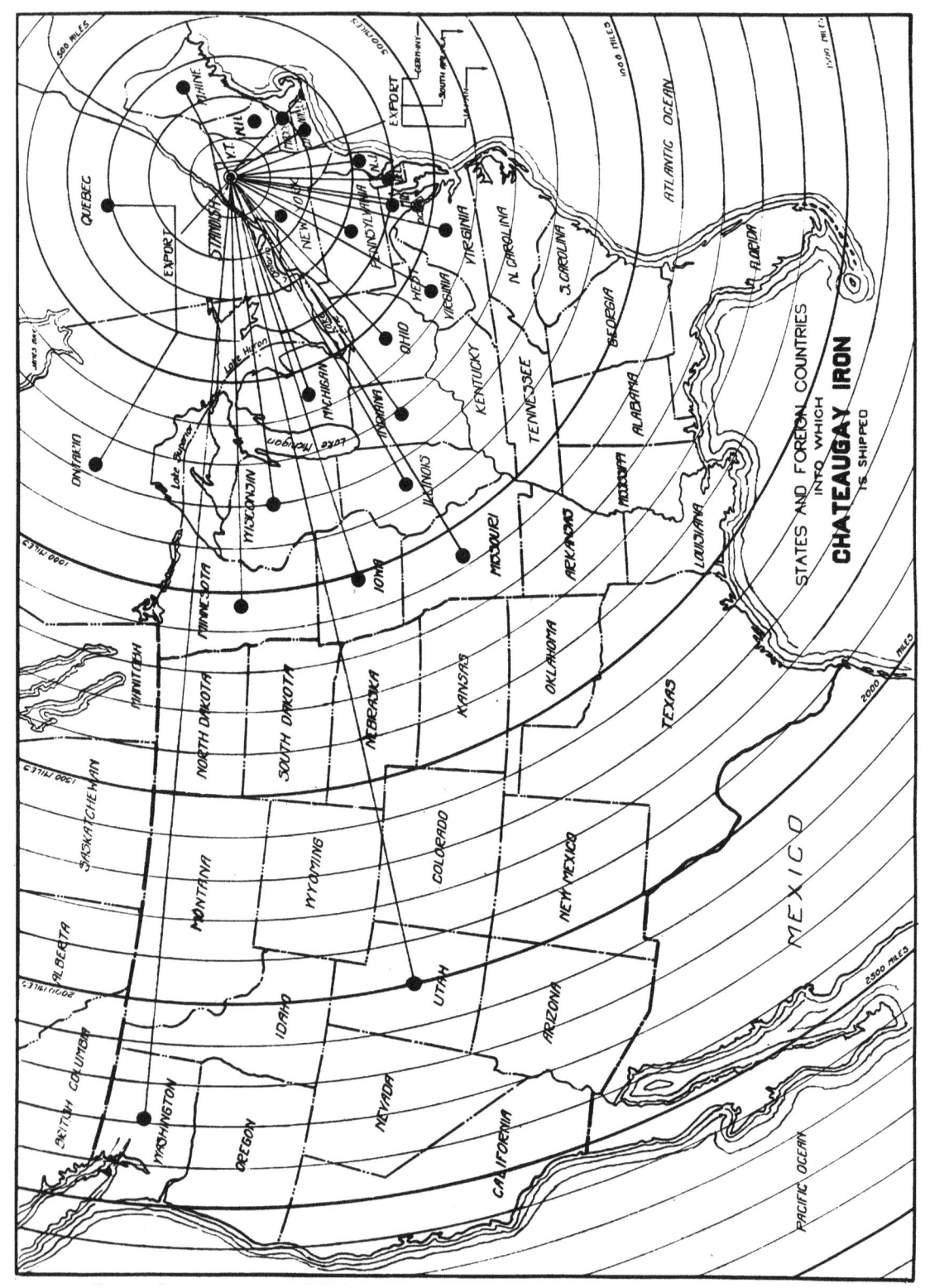

STATES AND FOREIGN COUNTRIES INTO WHICH CHATEAUGAY IRON IS SHIPPED

use as a mix or sweetener, with high phosphorus ores. It is also used in the open hearth puddling, and electric furnaces, for oxidizing purposes. It is also very desirable for making pure sponge iron by the direct process.

Chateaugay pig iron is used in the acid open hearth, crucible, electric, puddling and air furnaces and cupola processes, embracing such products as steel wire, cable, drill steel, steel forgings, car wheels, die blocks, rolls, cylinders, gears, springs, cams, shuttle races, piano plates, piston rings, crankshafts, chucks, steel and rolling mill equipment and many other types of machinery.

It is specially suitable in castings of intricate design where heavy and light sections meet and increased strength with hard wearing surfaces is desired.

It is extensively used in the production of all kinds of rolls.

Its freedom from phosphorus, together with other characteristics of this iron, helps to close the grain in pressure castings and prevent leakage. It has also been definitely proven that acid and heat resisting castings have prolonged life when made of this iron.

Its introduction among the gray iron foundries was considered a radical step, since it was not presumed that an iron, so well adapted for the production of high grade steel, could be effectively or economically utilized for gray iron. It was discovered, however, that it possessed certain working characteristics which heretofore seemed confined to charcoal iron only. Its comparative freedom from sulphur and phosphorus, and its richness in carbon, permit its use in the low silicon grades for closing the grain and increasing the strength, without penalty on machinability.

Many constant users of Chateaugay pig iron are of the firm opinion that it has certain characteristics and qualities, in addition to being extremely low in sulphur and phosphorus and free of copper, that cannot be found by chemical analyses in the ordinary laboratory.

Let us consider for a moment the electronic theory. A casting is made according to certain specifications and chemical analysis. It is then put into use, subjected to the shock and strain that its duty imposes upon it, and later on it breaks. If it has given average service it is scrapped without further comment, and usually replaced by another similar casting.

If the broken casting were sent to the laboratory for analysis, it is quite likely the same elements such as carbon, silicon, phosphorus, manganese, sulphur, etc., would be found, and unless it had been subjected to wear and abrasion it would be found to weigh as much as it did originally.

If the broken casting contains the same chemical analysis, has not lost any appreciable weight, and is properly designed and made, what causes it to break after performing its duty for a given length of time?

GEORGE WASHINGTON BRIDGE, HUDSON RIVER, N. Y. CITY
15,000 TONS OF CHATEAUGAY IRON USED TO MANUFACTURE THE STEEL CABLES

According to one of the electronic theories, the casting or metal has become fatigued, caused by the electrons going off into space during the performance of its duty. If this be so, it is plainly seen why the continued use of scrap over and over is bound to result in inferior castings. Inasmuch as the quality of scrap is such an unknown factor, it becomes more and more essential for the steel maker and foundryman to select the highest grade of pig iron obtainable for the base of his mixture.

From the results obtained by users of Chateaugay pig iron over a period of a great many years, there seems no doubt but that the Chateaugay ore (of which there is no other similar deposit to be found) contains either more or an exceptional combination of electrons, or both, than any other known ore, and that these exceptional features carry on into the iron through the process of refinement.

Iron ore tailings, by-products which are produced during the refinement of the concentrated ore by the concentrating plant, are sold in large quantities for the following uses: Both fine and coarse aggregates for concrete, plastering and mortar work, composition roofing, macadam, track ballast, locomotive and engine sand, filtering, sand blasting, filler, and as a slag forming material in the blast furnace. Its use is also being considered as flotation sand in the cone coal cleaning process, mineral surfaced asphalt bridge plant, abrasives, and ceramics.

Russell S. Greenman, Consulting Engineer, Albany, N. Y., an expert authority on concrete engineering, made an exhaustive study of these ore tailings as concrete aggregates a few years ago. His report shows this material to contain no loam or vegetable matter, nor any substance soluble in water, and that concrete made with it has from 17% to 24% more tensile and compressive strength than concrete made with Ottawa sand. Ottawa sand is generally used as a standard by all authorities on concrete.

Further, Mr. Greenman's report says, in part:

"Concrete is a variable product, and subject to much abuse in its making and in its use. To provide against the forces of nature and of man, concrete needs first of all to be made carefully and properly. Then it must be made of materials suitable for the uses to be made of the product. Strength in this product is an important factor, but the density of a material—either in itself or as a component part of concrete—is most vital if concrete is to be a permanent structural material.

"The test data of these examinations and tests show that these ore tailings, both sand and stone sizes, offer superior materials for use in concrete. Where density, durability, high strength, and surfaces able to withstand severe abrasive or weathering actions are desired they can be secured by the use of these materials. And too, for mass work the

DAM ON SARANAC RIVER, BUILT WITH CHATEAUGAY ORE TAILINGS

NEW YORK STATE CONCRETE HIGHWAY, BUILT WITH CHATEAUGAY ORE TAILINGS

SECTION OF D. & H. R. R. TRACK NEAR BLUFF POINT, BALLASTED WITH CHATEAUGAY ORE TAILINGS

UNDERPASS, D. & H. R. R. CHATEAUGAY ORE TAILINGS USED TO MAKE THE CONCRETE

HYDRO ELECTRIC POWER PLANT ON SARANAC RIVER, BUILT WITH ORE TAILINGS

INTERIOR POWER HOUSE, SARANAC RIVER, BUILT WITH ORE TAILINGS

36 INCH BELT CONVEYOR CARRYING ORE TAILINGS TO R. R. CARS FOR MARKET

CONCRETE HIGHWAY APPROACH TO OVERHEAD CROSSING, D. & H. R. R., WHITEHALL TUNNEL AND GRADE ELIMINATION. BUILT WITH CHATEAUGAY ORE TAILINGS

WHITEHALL TUNNEL AND GRADE ELIMINATION, D. & H. R. R., BUILT WITH CHATEAUGAY ORE TAILINGS

density and weight of concrete are important factors, and these materials produce these qualities; and for thin section work, such as slabs for example, the high strength producing quality of these materials offers an opportunity to safely reduce sections."

From 1925 to 1933, inclusive, 793,726 net tons of iron ore tailings were sold and shipped to market.

The products of the woodlands are sold for the following uses: Pulpwood manufacture, manufacture of novelties, fence posts, fuel, railroad ties, sawed lumber, mine props, transmission line poles, Christmas trees, and manufacturing excelsior.

While the revenue from the woodlands has not been very much since 1915, it is expected that, beginning with the year 1938, it will be very substantial, as a result of the growth to commercial maturity of many of the trees. During the last year, about 275 railroad cars of woodlands products were shipped to market, in addition to the products sold to individuals who transported them other than by rail.

Chapter VI

WOODLANDS AND FORESTS

Woodlands and Forests

The territory within which the Chateaugay Ore and Iron Company forests lie is representative of the hardwood and coniferous regions of the Adirondack Mountains of New York. This is true not only in respect to general forest conditions and climate, but also economic and social conditions.

Any history of Adirondack forest property which attempts to describe the mangement of forest property must necessarily connect the relation of forests with the development and settlement of this region during the 19th Century. This is especially apparent today when one considers that development of the Adirondacks depends entirely upon the mining, wood using and agricultural industries.

The early settlers, who pioneered the mountainous Adirondack region in Clinton and Franklin counties, west of Lake Champlain and the Champlain Valley, in the early part of the 19th Century, established small saw and grist mills and iron forges. The grist mills provided the necessities of life for the settlers, who in most instances penetrated through these regions to obtain the iron found over a wide and scattered area. Saw mills were erected to supply lumber for the building of homes and other building purposes in connection with the construction of iron forges.

The small iron forges first worked in the northern section of the Adirondack Mountains made no serious inroad upon the wood capital of the surrounding forest lands. Practically virgin forests existed, except for small areas cleared for agricultural and mining purposes until 1870. Prior to that date the mountainous regions of the Adirondacks were too remote for any extensive lumbering, although the many small iron forges, started between 1800 and 1870, were dependent entirely on the forest for obtaining charcoal and other wood supplies for smelting ore.

The iron industry in Clinton and Franklin counties gradually came into the hands of such prominent iron men as Smith M. Weed and Andrew Williams, who in 1873 originated and formed the Chateaugay Iron Company, starting with forges at Clayburg and Russia, in Clinton County, and at Belmont, in Franklin county. Other forges at numerous points in the counties aforementioned were subsequently constructed.

With the formation of the Chateaugay Iron Company in 1873, the managers and officers of this Company started acquisition of forest lands in the towns of Ellenburg, Dannemora, Saranac and Black Brook, Clinton County, and in the towns of Belmont and Franklin, Franklin County, in order to supply their numerous forges with a cheap and easily available source of charcoal. Charcoal kilns of various types, the last used being named the beehive kiln, were originally built on these forest lands in the vicinity of the forges. Later, with the development and construction of company-owned plank roads and the extension of railroad facilities of the Delaware and Hudson Canal Company, kilns were placed wherever an easily available supply of wood could be found. Purchases were continued until approximately 100,000 acres of timber land had been acquired. Records indicate that the bulk of these forest lands were purchased at tax sales by the State of New York. These acquisitions were, of course, aided and increased by direct purchases by additional tracts from individual owners. No records exist today that will tell us definitely the amount of wood taken from forest lands for conversion into charcoal, but it is known that at one time 101 charcoal kilns, with a yearly capacity of 1,000 cords each, were in operation, and it is also known that for thirty years the Chateaugay Company and its predecessors made iron with charcoal produced from its forest acreage. It is estimated that over 1,500,000 cords or roughly 135,000,000 cubic feet of wood were used for this purpose alone. In addition to this use of the forest, large sawmills were erected by the Company at various points to furnish lumber and wood supplies to erect homes and other buildings needed for the mining and manufacture of iron. The cutting of wood for charcoal purposes was continued until 1904, when coke was introduced to replace the use of charcoal.

In 1896, to increase revenue from these forest lands, a contract was entered into with the Glens Falls Paper Mill Company, later known as the International Pulp and Paper Company, whereby the Paper Company agreed to purchase yearly 15,000 cords of four foot spruce and balsam pulpwood. This contract remained in force until about 1915, when the entire Chateaugay holdings were about cleared of wood, suitable for this purpose. Although records fail to give the complete story of lumbering operations on lands included in the Chateaugay Ore and Iron Company forest, verbal evidence leads us to believe that the Chateaugay Company management in 1896, held certain wise and far sighted opinions on the management of this forest. It can be noted with considerable satisfaction that, in entering into this agreement on the cutting of pulpwood, the Chateaugay Company sold only down to a 10" D. B. H. (diameter breast high) limit, and that employees engaged in overseeing the cutting of the Glens Falls Company were careful in following out this contract condition. This practice must have been based on the experience obtained in cutting wood for charcoal, wherein it was found impracticable to completely cut the forest lands.

In 1903, the Delaware and Hudson Company, after acquiring the Chateaugay and Lake Placid Railway Company, secured control of the Chateaugay Ore and Iron Company, seemingly with the view of increasing the mining and smelting operations at Lyon Mountain and Standish and, subsequently, freight movements on its railroad lines. Shortly after these acquisitions, during the Summer and Fall of 1903, destructive forest fires burned over approximately three-fourths of the Chateaugay Company's forest. A portion of the acreage, burned clean of timber, was later considered as entirely denuded. The major portion of the burned area was probably affected by serious ground fires, which did not entirely damage the remaining stands of timber, but necessitated placing this timber on an early market. The forest fires of 1903 were the first to seriously affect the Chateaugay Company's property.

Due to the destructive forest fires of that year, the Chateaugay Company in September, 1904, entered into a contract with the Dock and Coal Company, of Plattsburg, New York, under which the last named Company purchased all the remaining merchantable hardwood and conifers not covered by contract with the Glens Falls Company. This contract also provided that lumbering for the Glens Falls Company would be done by the Dock and Coal Company, the Chateaugay Company to receive payment on a stumpage basis. Along with the extensive lumbering of the Dock and Coal Company, forest fires continued to eat into the Company's forest lands. In the same year that stumpage was contracted with the Dock and Coal Company, Thomas H. Sherrard, of the United States Bureau of Forestry, made a preliminary survey of the Chateaugay Ore and Iron Company's Adirondack timber lands at the request of the officials of the Chateaugay Company. In Sherrard's examination of the Chateaugay forest holdings, it was shown that, in 1904, forest properties of the Chateaugay Company could be classified as follows:

1. Virgin spruce and hardwoods — 18,000 acres
2. Virgin hardwoods with some spruce — 17,000 "
3. Virgin hardwoods without spruce — 10,000 "
4. Second growth (on which another crop of various hardwood species was mature and ready for cutting) — 23,000 "
5. Denuded or brush lands — 28,000 "

Lands of the Chateaugay Company used in connection with mining and agricultural purposes were not included in Sherrard's classification. The agricultural lands in 1904 were those cleared by wood contractors around their various operations to aid in supplying yearly food requirements.

Sherrard in his report to the officers of the Chateaugay Company, recommended a reforesting program for the denuded lands, and suggestions for decreasing the possibility of future forest fires. After considering this matter, the Company followed Sherrard's recommendations and decided to reforest the 28,000 acres that were considered in 1904 as denuded lands.

The first tree nursery established was located at Wolf Pond in Franklin County, in the section in which it was decided reforestation should be commenced. This nursery started raising seedlings and transplant trees of White and Scotch pine, Norway spruce, and European larch. Various species were apparently experimented with to determine the most suitable for the section to be planted. It was known, of course, that certain pines, firs, and hardwoods were native to the Adirondacks, but the Scotch pine tree belonged to a European specie of pine grown extensively and with good results in Germany and Russia. No one raising forest trees in nurseries in 1906 knew much about this work and consequently the number of seedlings raised was limited. Damping off became one of the largest of nursery troubles, not only at Wolf Pond but in all the State nurseries. Not until many years later was a simple but effective remedy found to offset it. This nursery, about 1,500 feet above sea level, was abandoned after the field planting operations of 1915, as it was found that trees could not be dug out for planting purposes until late in the Spring, the season at Wolf Pond being some two weeks later in opening than around Lake Champlain, which is only about one hundred feet above sea level. In the meantime, another nursery had been located at Bluff Point, near Plattsburg, about 1910, and it soon became apparent that this location was an ideal site. White and Scotch pine still continued to be the standard trees raised for planting, although such species as White cedar, White ash, Norway spruce and Black locust were raised to some extent. It was undoubtedly estimated that the nurseries should supply each year approximately 1,000,000 trees, or enough to reforest 1,000 acres. It was soon found difficult to meet this requirement.

Forest fires continued burning the Chateaugay Forest year after year. These fires, most severe in 1903, 1908, 1911, 1913, and 1915, destroyed practically all timber that was ready for market and scorched the ground so badly that the humus, needed by the soil to establish another ground-cover of valuable hard and soft woods, was burned down to sand and stones, on which a fire cover of inferior woods began to grow in order to assist nature in enriching the soil cover. The Dock and Coal Company continued cutting in the burned areas from which salvage could be obtained, and from the lands which had not been burned until 1918, when operations ceased as the timber supply was exhausted. There remaining only scattered areas of cull hardwoods that had been lumbered once and burned over several times. Other than such hardwoods, nothing remained but undersized swamp balsam and spruce which, because of its location in wet areas, had not been badly burned.

SEED BEDS AND TRANSPLANTS OF VARIOUS SPECIES AND AGES AT THE BLUFF POINT NURSERY IN 1921

TYPE OF AREAS DENUDED BY FOREST FIRES AT WOLF POND IN FRANKLIN COUNTY. FOREGROUND REFORESTED IN 1915 WITH SCOTCH PINE. 1910 SCOTCH PINE PLANTATION IN BACKGROUND

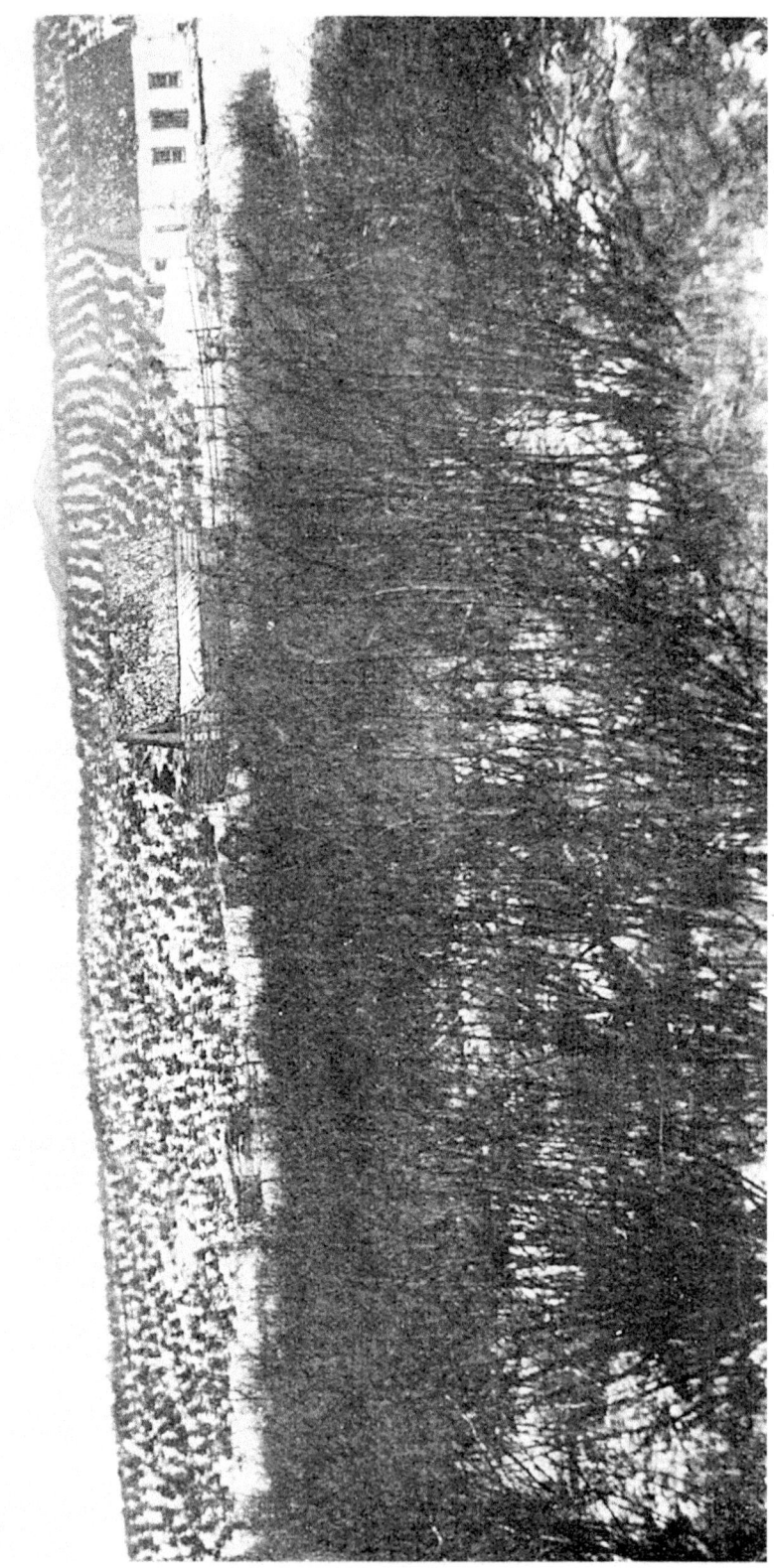

A VIEW OF THE 1910 SCOTCH PINE PLANTATION AT MIDDLE KILNS IN FRANKLIN COUNTY, PHOTOGRAPHED IN 1915. ALDER SWAMP IN FOREGROUND ALONG MIDDLE KILNS BROOK

In 1915, the White pine in the Bluff Point Nursery began to be troubled with blister rust. While every precaution was taken to control and eradicate this disease, it became necessary, in 1917, to destroy all White pine in this nursery to help check the spread of this disease which caused great damage throughout the State of New York. Subsequent to 1917, no White pine was carried in the nursery for any purpose, and the trend in specie changed to the raising of as much Red pine as possible, the seed of which was hard to obtain, even in limited quantities. Scotch pine, with some White and Norway spruce, was also grown in large quantities. Numerous other species, including Douglas spruce, Austrian pine, Montana pine, Western Yellow or Bull pine, White willow, Norway poplar, Engleman spruce, Concolor fir, White ash, European larch, Dwarf Mountain pine, Balsam fir, and Colorado Blue spruce, were still experimented with, although throughout the time reforesting was carried on, nothing practical was discovered other than the pines and spruces listed immediately above.

The planting of the trees raised in the nurseries first began in 1908, when 18,000 Scotch pine trees were set out at Wolf Pond. Each year thereafter until 1927, the last planting year, reforestation was carried on with the exception only of the years 1909, 1911, and 1919. In 1913, when reforesting had just begun to be well started and some 1,100 acres had been planted to Scotch and White pine, there was estimated to be 40,900 acres of burned and denuded land suitable for stocking with trees. The forest cover changed rapidly, however, and the planting of 1927 cleaned up practically all available areas. After the 1927 program, about 12,500 acres, on which some 14,764,846 trees had been planted, constituted the reforested area. The remaining 28,400 acres, originally estimated in 1913 as plantable land, had grown up to hardwood brush under which it was not feasible to start artificial reproduction of pine or spruce.

At various periods following Sherrard's examination for forest conditions, estimates were made of the remaining stands of scattered timber. One estimate, made in 1918 after all lumbering operations had ceased, is given here to indicate conditions at that time. This report shows that only 19,952 acres were covered with timber of any size, and that on this acreage there were 136,639,844 board feet of hardwoods, of which only a small percentage could be made into merchantable lumber because of the poor quality of the timber, which unquestionably had been lumbered through at least once by the Dock and Coal Company. In addition to the hardwoods, there were 8,072 cords of poplar and 13,859,775 board feet of spruce, balsam, hemlock and cedar, of which only 7,181,078 board feet were available for market, the remainder being too scattered and of poor quality.

In 1920 and 1921, field data were obtained for the preparation of a twenty-year working plan. Crews, under the supervision of Professors

PHOTOGRAPH, TAKEN IN 1915, OF THE NORTHERLY PORTION OF THE 1910 SCOTCH PINE PLANTATION SOUTH OF WOLF POND IN THE SALMON RIVER VALLEY

A VIEW OF THE 1912 SCOTCH PINE PLANTATION AT WOLF POND IN FRANKLIN COUNTY ESTABLISHED UNDER A SMALL GROWTH OF POPLAR AND CHERRY AS PHOTOGRAPHED IN 1915

1915 RED PINE PLANTATION SOUTH OF WOLF POND IN FRANKLIN COUNTY

Spring, Bently and Guise, of the College of Forestry of Cornell University, worked over the entire woodland holdings of the Company, which had increased by this time to 120,684 acres, the major portion of this land being located in townships 3, 4, 5, 8 and 9, Old Military Tract, in Clinton and Franklin counties. The location of the Company boundary lines had been established in 1911, 1912, and 1913 by surveys which had been made in order to develop a typographical map of the property. These surveys were of great assistance to the Cornell crew. Professor Spring made a study of silvicultural conditions and laid out permanent sample plots in each of the recognized growth types encountered. Growth studies were in charge of Professor Bently, who obtained data for figuring stand, growth, and volume tables. Professor Guise conducted the timber survey and used the strip system. Where the tree growth was such as to warrant, 10% estimates were made and all trees in the strip calipered. In other cases, strips were run at one quarter mile intervals and estimates made by the use of one-tenth acre circles.

Conclusions arrived at from this field work indicate that, of the entire Chateaugay forest holdings in 1921, 87,724 acres could not be considered as growing any timber or wood supplies that would in any way be merchantable within the twenty-year period, ending in July, 1941. This acreage included reforested lands and areas of small second growth. Of the 32,960 acres, from which some revenue could be expected, 22,749 acres were covered, in part, by a stand of poplar estimated by the Cornell foresters as being capable of producing approximately 100,000 cords between 1937 and 1941.

The 12,500 acres of Chateaugay reforestation is today in excellent condition. This reforestation comprises, in most part, areas set out in Scotch pine, Red pine and White pine. The older Scotch pine plantations contain trees between thirty and thirty-five feet high, and an estimated percentage of living trees in all Scotch pine plantations averages about 80%. Individual trees run up to nine inches in diameter, measured breast high, although the average pines in our 1908, 1910 and 1912 plantations run about six inches Percentage of catch, or percentage showing the estimated amount of living trees in these plantations, run from fifty per cent for the poorer areas to ninety per cent in what was considered as the best types of planting soil and conditions The earlier Scotch pine plantations are now rapidly approaching a condition where extensive thinnings will be necessary. In addition to the thinnings needed, lateral branches must be pruned to clear the boles or trunks of these trees to improve butt logs for lumber. The work of thinning these plantations is being held up until it can be found possible to do this work at a minimum expense. The thinnings should, in large part, pay for themselves from the salvage that may be obtained. Hardwoods have in numerous cases encroached upon some of the later planted areas so that weeding of undesirable species is now necessary to permit rapid growth of the reforested stock.

Property acquisitions continued until 1928, when the total area of Chateaugay Company lands reached about 150,000 acres. These recent acquisitions were made, some by purchase from individuals and others by County and State tax sales. About 6,500 acres cover farm and forest lands, purchased along the Saranac River in Clinton County, but the bulk of the later purchases included forest lands in different stages of growth, most of which had been lumbered over many times. These properties for the most part are located in townships 3, 4, 8, 9, Old Military Tract and the Refugee Tract, just east of the Military Tract. The Parmalee lands, purchased in 1925, increased the Company holdings by about 7,748 acres and also included some 20,000 acres of mineral rights in Franklin County.

It is generally difficult to accurately forecast expected revenues from forest properties, as fires, insects, disease and weather conditions have in the past usually upset expectations of forest yield, but the indications today are that, before many years, the earlier reforested areas of this Company's woodlands will be on a self-sustaining basis for a considerable period of time, and will bring substantial revenue to its owners and increased freight business to The Delaware and Hudson Railroad.

Appendix

CHRONOLOGY OF IRON AND STEEL (IN PART)

Chronology of Iron and Steel (*in part*)

PREHISTORIC TIMES

Egypt

It is believed that the three oldest pieces of wrought iron in existence are a sickle blade found by Belzoni under the base of a sphinx in Karnac, near Thebes; a blade, probably 5,000 years old, found by Colonel Yvse in one of the pyramids; and a portion of a crosscut saw which must have been made earlier than 880 B. C., exhumed by Layard at Nimrod.

W. M. Flinders Petrie states that iron was known in Egypt from the middle of the prehistoric civilization—about 7000 to 6000 B. C.—onward. He found a shapeless iron mass, surrounded by bronze tools, dating from the Sixth Dynasty, about 2600 B. C.

Asia Minor

In Asia Minor, inland from Troy and the Aegean world, there lived from before the time of Hammurapi, 2000 B. C., a great group of white peoples which built up there about 1500 B. C. a powerful empire. They are called the Hittites. These people began working the iron ore deposits along the Black Sea before the Thirteenth Century B. C., and became the earliest distributors of iron. This was the time when iron began to displace bronze in the Mediterranean world and the East. It was through contact with the Hittites that iron was introduced into Assyria; and the Assyrian forces were the first large armies equipped with weapons of iron. A single arsenal room in the palace of Sargon II, who had raised Assyria to the height of her grandeur about 705 B. C., contained 200 tons of iron implements.

China

The oldest notice of the use of iron in China appears in the "Yu Kung," which may be called the geographical section of the "Book of History," and dates from 2200 B. C. Iron was then obtained in the province of Szechuen, in the region where salt and natural gas are now worked by deep borings.

Ancient Britain

The Britons were familiar with iron before the invasion of Julius Caesar in 55 B. C. They used scythes on their war chariots; and slag remains found in the Cheviot Hills and elsewhere have been shown to be of date prior to that time.

ANCIENT AMERICA

Foster, in his "Prehistoric Races of the United States of America," says that "no implement of iron has been found in connection with the ancient civilization of America."

Professor Putnam states: "I have found in the ancient mounds of Ohio, masses of meteoric iron and various implements and ornaments made by hammering pieces of meteoric iron.—None of our peoples, I am confident, understood smelting iron or in any way manufacturing it from iron ore:"

A tribe near the mouth of the Rio de La Plata, in South America, had arrows tipped with meteoric iron.

Jose de Acosta, a Spanish missionary and author of the Sixteenth Century, mentions wedge-shaped pieces of iron circulated as currency in Paraguay. The Aztecs also possessed knives, daggers, etc., made of meteoric iron.

EARLIEST HISTORICAL PERIOD

B. C. 507

The Etruscan king, Porsenna, was victor in a war against Rome, and in the conditions of peace prohibited Romans from using iron except for agricultural purposes.

B. C. 340

Daimachus, a writer of the Fourth Century, B. C., enumerated four kinds of steel and their uses: Chalybdic and Synoptic for ordinary tools; Lydian for swords, razors, and surgical instruments; and Lacedaemonian for files, augers, chisels, and stone-cutting implements. This was in the time of Alexander the Great.

B. C. 322

According to Aristotle, who wrote in the Fourth Century, B. C., the Chalybians made iron from sand ore dug from river banks, washed, and put into a furnace along with the stone Pyrimachus (fire maker), that is, coal.

Aristotle seems further to indicate that cast iron as well as steel was known in his time: "Wrought iron itself may be cast so as to be made liquid and to harden again; and thus it is they are wont to make steel." He described also the process of making Indian steel called "wootz," which was made in crucibles.

The metal for the famous Damascus weapons was made at Kona Samundrum, Hyderabad, India, and was carried by Persian merchants to Damascus. The ore was carefully selected, washed, and roasted if necessary, then reduced with charcoal in small fire clay crucibles and allowed to cool in the crucibles.

Next it was subjected to a tempering process, consisting of repeated heating while covered with an iron oxide paste to soften it to suit the desire of the purchaser, who regularly watched the operation throughout. The ores used were very free from both sulphur and phosphorus and contained but little copper.

It appears that at a later period metal for the Damascus trade was made also at Toledo, Spain. Toledo was captured by the Romans in 192 B. C. and from that time, together with other places in Spain, supplied the Romans with swords.

B. C. 200

Iron currency bars were in use in England during the period known as La Tenae, i. e. the Second Century B. C.

The embrasures for cannon constructed in the great wall of China, built about this time, furnish proof that the Chinese used artillery in this epoch. But little is indicated as to what kind of artillery it was.

CHRISTIAN ERA

First Century

Pliny the Elder, a Roman author whose "Natural History" was published about 77 A. D., describes the various kinds of iron and steel which were in use in his day: "Howbeit, as many kinds of iron as there be, none shall match in goodness the steel that comes from the Seres. In a second degree of goodness may be placed the Parthian iron."

The old district of Franchimont in Belgium possessed rich deposits of iron in the midst of vast forests, and metallurgical industries flourished there in the first centuries of the Christian Era.

Second Century

The year after the Roman emperor Hadrian landed in Britain, there was established at Bath, Wiltshire, a Roman military "fabrica" for the manufacture of iron arms. This was close to the bloomeries in Somerset and to the Forest of Dean, which supplied them with iron.

310

The carved iron pillar at Delhi, India, bears an inscription in Sanskrit describing it as a "triumphal pillar of Rajah Dhava, A. D. 310, who wrote his immortal fame with his sword." This appears to be the whole record of his fame, a writing far more permanent than that of his sword. This pillar, which is 16 inches in diameter by 24 feet long, seems to have been made up of blooms of very nearly pure wrought iron of about eighty pounds weight each, which were welded together into the pillar. Hadfield's analysis of samples from this pillar showed: carbon 0.08%, silicon 0.046%, sulphur 0.006%, phosphorus 0.114%, manganese nil, iron (by analysis) 99.72%.

321

There is another larger pillar from the same period at Dhar, the ancient capital of Malava. This was at least 42 feet long. There are also in existence in India several very large iron girders at Puri, ornamental iron gates of ancient origin at Somnali, and a wrought iron piece, gun or engine of some kind, said to be 24 feet in length, at Nuwiri.

Roman Occupation of Britain, 55 B. C. to 409 A. D.

During the Roman occupation of Britain, and also much later, iron was obtained in a malleable state, with charcoal as fuel, directly from the ore by a process much like the Catalan process. The ore was mixed with charcoal and strongly heated in a simple hearth, using a single tuyere, the air being blown by bellows. The product could be made either very soft or steely hard, according to the way the operation was conducted. The metal, however, was not very uniform from one operation to the next, and there was a large loss of iron in the slag.

Eighth Century in General

At about the beginning of the Eighth Century the iron industry took a fresh start in many European countries and experienced what in modern phraseology we term a "revival."

When the Moors became masters of much of Spain in the early part of the century, they greatly stimulated the manufacture of iron. The natives who had withstood the Moors, also extended their Catalan forges north into France and even to other European countries. So prominent did the iron industry of Spain become, that its ironworkers were sought by other countries; and on the French side of the Pyrenees, in the mountains of Germany and along the Rhine, many of their small forges were erected.

The early part of the Eighth Century seems to have been the period when the "wolf furnaces" or "Stuckofen" or "loup furnaces"—all of which terms refer to the same kind of furnace—were introduced into most of the European iron districts. The wolf furnace was a high bloomery, and was simply an enlargement of the primitive low bloomeries or forges, somewhat like a Catalan forge, extending upward to some ten feet in height in the form of a quadrangular or circular shaft about two feet wide at top and bottom and five feet at the widest part. There was an opening in front about two feet square, called the breast, and the blast was applied from at least two bellows and nozzles, both on the same side. They existed in Nassau, where iron of great celebrity was made by a guild of forest smiths; also in Siegen, Saxony, and the Hartz Mountains, all of which are located in the territory covered by modern Germany. They were also in use in the Austrian provinces of Styria, Carinthia, and Carniola.

TENTH CENTURY IN GENERAL

The Anglo-Saxon monks frequently engaged in the manufacture of iron. St. Dunstan, who lived in the Tenth Century, is said to have had a forge in his bedroom and to have been a skilled blacksmith and metallurgist.

MEDIAEVAL PERIOD

1066

William the Conqueror won the battle of Hastings largely because his soldiers were better armed than those of the Saxon, Harold.

The smith in England at this time was treated as an officer of the highest rank because of the dependence on him for arms and armor. The forging of swords was his great specialty. The manufacture of defensive armor had been brought to such a high state of perfection that it was said "a knight completely armed was almost invulnerable."

1264

The oldest iron manufacture in Japan was at Sugaya, from magnetic sands.

THIRTEENTH CENTURY IN GENERAL

The oldest iron mine in Sweden is probably Norberg, which was worked at least as early as the Thirteenth Century. It is situated in Westmanland, on the southern borders of Dalecarlia.

RENAISSANCE PERIOD

1340

The blast furnace originated in the Rhine provinces of Prussia about the beginning of the Fourteenth Century. Swank says: "We are unable to trace its existence to an earlier date than 1340, when the furnace at Marche les Dames, in Belgium, was built."

1355

An act was passed in England to provide that no iron should be carried out of the country, either iron made in England or that imported and sold there.

FOURTEENTH CENTURY IN GENERAL

Chaucer, the English poet, wrote of the "Sheffield whittle" as being in common use in the Fourteenth Century. Sheffield was then already famous for its cutlery.

1488

The celebrated Dannemora mines in Sweden were opened.

EARLY HISTORICAL PERIOD

1543

The first British cast-iron cannon were made by Ralph Hogge at Bucksteed, in Sussex, England, he being assisted by the same Peter Baude who invented shells. The shells were made by Peter van Cullen, a Belgian.

1550

The wooden bellows used in blowing blast furnaces was invented about this year by Hans Lobsinger, an organist at Nuremberg.

1556

Georgius Agricola, sometimes styled "the Father of Metallurgy," was by far the most important metallurgical author of the Sixteenth Century. His great book on this subject was published in Latin after his death by Froben at Basel in the year 1556. This book seems to have been in preparation during a period of over twenty years. He apparently completed it in 1550, but did not send it to press until 1553, and it did not appear until a year after his death in 1555. He was not merely an author, but was a man of considerable importance in many public affairs of his time and occupied repeatedly important posts of public authority. In De Re Metallica he described for the first time in an intelligent and detailed way scores of methods and processes which represent the accumulation of generations of experience and knowledge. His book was not excelled for nearly two centuries, and its value to the men who followed in his profession can scarcely be gauged.

1558

The iron works in England were consuming the forests for fuel so rapidly that great fear was felt of a scarcity of wood for naval purposes. This led to the passage, in the first year of the reign of Elizabeth, of an act designed to prevent the use of timber for fuel in iron manufacture. A still more stringent act was passed a few years later.

1585

Iron ore was discovered in a number of places in North Carolina by an expedition sent out by Sir Walter Raleigh.

COLONIAL PERIOD

1608

Iron ore was first exported from the American colonies by the Virginia Company, near Jamestown, the ore being smelted in England and the iron sold to the East India Company for £4 per ton.

Forks were introduced into England in this year.

1613
      Rovenson invented the reverberatory furnace, which he described as follows: "bloomeries, fineries and chafferies of division in which the material to be melted or wrought may be kept divided from touch of the fewels."

1619
      The Virginia Company sent John Berkeley, "a gentleman of honorable family," of Beverstone Castle, Gloucestershire, with a company of 22 skilled ironworkers to "set up three ironworks in the colony." They built a forge at Falling Creek, Va., 66 miles above Jamestown. Ore was secured from pits two miles above the plant, on the creek, and from a bog, the "iron bottom," about a half mile south.

      Dud Dudley, of Worcester, England, obtained from King James a patent relating to smelting iron ore with pit or sea coal. He made the first iron at Pensnett Chase, in Worcestershire, and refined it "into merchantable good bar iron" there and at Cradley forges. Dudley's furnace was larger than was then usual. He used very large bellows, and thus succeeded in making about seven tons of pig iron per week. A combination of charcoal ironmasters opposed the innovation and forced Dudley out of one enterprise after another, so that his discovery was not very profitable for him financially. However, he continued making iron with pit coal, more or less regularly, for nearly fifty years.

1622
      The Virginia Company's enterprise at Falling Creek, Va., continued prosperously until March 22, 1622, when it was destroyed by the Indians and all the workmen were massacred, only John Berkeley's young son escaping. The plant was not rebuilt.

1630
      Master Beaumont substituted for the common road a railroad with wooden tram rails from his coal pits near Newcastle, England, to the riverside. When the draft was harder than usual in consequence of a steep ascent or a sharp curve in the line, friction was diminished by nailing to the wooden rails thin plates of malleable iron.

1645
      The first successful iron enterprise in the American colonies was at Lynn, Mass. Eleven "English gentlemen" supplied some five thousand dollars capital, and Governor Winthrop's son furnished political influence. Many special privileges were secured, such as a monopoly of iron making in Lynn for 21 years, exemption from taxes for 20 years, exemption from all military service, a free gift of three square miles of land for every furnace built, etc. The first furnace made about eight tons of pig iron per week from neighboring bog ore.

The first iron casting made in America was a kettle of about one quart capacity, cast in Lynn, presumably from the earliest operation of this furnace. It was given to Thomas Hudson, younger brother of Hendrick Hudson, the explorer, as part consideration for 60 acres of land.

1650

The first official report of American-made iron being exported to England in the regular course of commerce reads as follows: "1650. Sam Hutchinson, merchant, shipped on the ship Charles 3½ tunne, 172 bars of iron for acco. of Ri. Hutchinson, of London." This iron was probably made at Lynn, Mass.

1651

The English were the first to substitute coke for charcoal in smelting operations in the Western world, although coking had been carried on in China long before this date. The first patent in this connection was granted to Jeremiah Buck.

1658

Captain Thomas Clarke, in company with John Winthrop and others, put in operation an "ironworks" at New Haven, Conn. This enterprise embraced a blast furnace and a refinery forge. This works was established at New Haven because of an offer by the Assembly of New Haven to any one who would establish ironworks there to exempt such an enterprise from paying taxes.

1666 or 1667

Wiredrawing was one of the early industries introduced into America at or near Lynn, Mass., very likely by Joseph Jenks. Charcoal iron was rolled into plates and the plates sheared into strips of square rods to form the raw material for drawing. This was the general practice of wire making until after Cort's grooved rolls came into use for rod making.

1674

The first ironworks in New Jersey were established at Tinton Falls, Shrewsbury, by Henry Leonard, previously of Raynham, Mass., and "made good iron, which is of great benefit to the country."

1685

Cast-iron water pipes were first made, and used at the water works at Versailles, France.

1703

Mordecai Lincoln was a large contributor to the erection of a forge at Bound Brook, N. J. This works made iron direct from the ore. His son, Mordecai Lincoln, Jr., who settled in Berks County, Pa., was the great-great-grandfather of Abraham Lincoln.

1710
> The earliest settlers at Hanover, N. J., located there "for the purpose of smelting iron ores in the neighborhood." Ore from the Succassunna Mine, later known as the Dickerson Mine, "was carried to the works in leather bags on pack horses, and the bar iron was carried on horseback over the Orange Mountains to Newark. The ore was, for some time, free to all."

1716
> The first ironworks in Pennsylvania of which any record has been preserved was a bloomery forge located on Manatawny Creek in Berks County, about three miles above Pottstown. This was started by Thomas Rutter, an English Quaker, and named Pool Forge. It is said to have produced a grade of iron better than the Swedish. This forge was attacked by the Indians in 1728, but they were repulsed.

1720
> The first blast furnace built in Pennsylvania was the Colebrookdale. A company composed of Thomas Rutter, James Lewis, Anthony Morris and others built this furnace on Ironstone Creek in Colebrookdale township, Berks County, about eight miles north of Pottstown. Plenty of cinder is said still to mark the exact spot.

1728
> Pennsylvania exported 274 tons of pig iron to Great Britain in this year.
>
> The manufacture of steel in America was first started in Connecticut. Samuel Higley of Simsbury, and Joseph Dewey of Hebron, claimed to have been the first in America to convert bar iron into steel. They made excellent steel, though in small quantities only.

1732
> Bituminous coal was first used in a blast furnace in America at Spotswood furnace, at Massaponas, below Fredericksburg, Va.
>
> Augustine Washington, father of George Washington, was largely interested in Accokeek furnace on the Rappahannock River in Stafford County, Va., which had been built by the Principio Company. He furnished ore to this furnace from his plantation two miles away.

1734
> C. E. Godfrey states that the first steelworks in America was established at Trenton on or before September 5, for the manufacture of various kinds of edge tools.
>
> As early as this a bloomery forge was erected by Thomas Lamb at Lime Rock in Litchfield County, Conn., which produced from 500 to 700 pounds of iron per day. A blast furnace was afterwards added to this forge.

1740

Mining of iron ore at Cornwall Ore Hills, Lebanon County, Pa., started in this year.

The first ironworks in the State of New York was built on Ancram Creek, Columbia County, about fourteen miles east of the Hudson River. This was erected by Philip Livingston, whose son, Robert R. Livingston, was one of the signers of the Declaration of Independence. This plant included both a blast furnace and a refinery forge. Most of the ore was obtained from the "Ore Hill" in Connecticut, about twelve miles from the works.

1742

Benjamin Franklin invented the open-front househeating stove which is still widely used and known as the "Franklin" stove.

The Oxford blast furnace, at Oxford, N. J., the first blast furnace in the Highlands of New Jersey, was started by Jonathan Robeson. It used charcoal fuel and was probably blown by a blast produced by water power. This furnace was still in operation in 1880, using anthracite.

Peter Grub, who had discovered the Cornwall ore deposit, Lebanon County, Pa., several years earlier, built the Cornwall furnace. The output was some twenty-five to thirty tons of iron per week, about four hundred bushels of charcoal being consumed in producing a ton of hammered bar iron from the ore. Partly because of low water in Summer, and partly because of the hot weather, the furnace was generally idle for about four months each year. The Cornwall bellows was of very large size, being 20 feet, 7 inches long, 5 feet, 10 inches wide across the breech, and 14 inches wide at the insertion of the nozzle.

1750

Cast-iron wheels were introduced for railed-road wagon use, at first on the forward axles only, in the belief that brakes would not hold on iron; but this was soon disproved, and all wheels were made of cast iron.

An act was passed by Parliament in Great Britain prohibiting the refining of pig iron or the manufacture of anything from it in the American colonies. The important points of this injunction were that no more rolling slitting mills, tilt hammer forges, and steel furnaces were to be built in America. American pig iron might be taken to England, duty free, but only to the port of London.

A vein of magnetic ore was discovered on Sterling Mountain in Orange County, N. Y. The next year Ward and Colton built a furnace there, the charcoal used being transported several miles on horseback on account of the lack of roads at that time. Two years later Abel Noble of Bucks County, Pa., erected a forge in Monroe, near the Sterling furnace. The anchors for the United States frigate "Constitution" were made here and also the anchors for the first ships of war that carried the Stars and Stripes.

1762

Colonel Ethan Allen, with whom were associated John Haseltiner and Samuel Forbes, built the first blast furnace in Connecticut at Lakeville, then called "Furnace Village," in Litchfield County.

1763

George Ross, a lawyer of Lancaster, Pa., and Mark Bird, of Philadelphia, built in West Manheim township, in the extreme southwestern part of York County, Pa., the first blast furnace established in Pennsylvania west of the Susquehanna River. George Ross was one of the signers of the Declaration of Independence.

1770

In this year the American Colonies exported 6,017 tons of pig iron, valued at $145,628; 2,463 tons of bar iron, valued at $178,891; two tons of castings, valued at $158; and eight tons of wrought iron valued at $810.

The first coke furnace was started in South Wales.

1775

About this year a few bloomeries were erected in Maine and Vermont. A few furnaces were afterwards erected in both states, and many bloomeries in Vermont. All have since disappeared.

REVOLUTIONARY WAR PERIOD

1777

New Jersey passed an act, October 7, 1777, "exempting from military service men to be employed at Mt. Hope and Hibernia furnaces, and reciting the necessity of providing the Army and Navy of the United States with cannon, cannon shot, etc."

1778

A great chain weighing 180 tons was made by Peter Townsend at the Sterling Iron Works, some twenty-five miles from West Point, N. Y. This chain was nearly a mile long, its links made of iron bars $2\frac{1}{2}$ inches square and weighing about one hundred pounds each. The manufacture of this chain was a great achievement, as it was accomplished in six weeks, 60 men being employed and 17 forges kept going night and day. It was stretched across the Hudson River at West Point, being supported by large logs about sixteen feet long, sharpened at the ends and set a short distance apart. The British vessels did not pass West Point. Other chains were stretched across the Hudson during the war to obstruct their passage, one of which, however, was destroyed by the British.

PERIOD OF SCIENTIFIC DEVELOPMENT

1787

Jonathan Leonard, of Canton, Mass. erected at Easton, Mass., a steel furnace "capable of making three tons at a batch." This was continued until 1808, and steel was made in considerable amounts. By this time commercial conditions required a larger furnace, and a ten-ton furnace was built. This produced cemented steel.

1790

Jacob Perkins, of Newburyport, Mass., invented a nail-cutting machine. This was patented five years later and was speedily followed by other inventions for the same purpose, some twenty-three patents being issued in the period from 1790 to 1800.

Previous to this time many country people in Massachusetts had little forges in their chimney corners and made nails in the winter evenings when little else could be done, even the children being sometimes thus occupied.

The first blast furnace west of the Alleghany Mountains was erected by William Turnbull and Peter Marmie, of Philadelphia, on the south side of Jacobs Creek, $2\frac{1}{2}$ miles above its junction with the Youghiogheny, in Fayette County, Pa. This was called the Alliance ironworks, and consisted of a furnace and a forge. The furnace was blown in November 1, 1790, and the iron was tried in the forge on the same day. This works continued in more or less regular operation for about twelve years.

1800

The price of hammered bar iron in the United States at this time was from $100 to $105 per long ton and the price of charcoal pig iron about $35.75. Statistics as to the tonnage of pig iron, bar iron and steel produced in this country seem not to be available for years earlier than 1810.

1802

In 1802 there were about one hundred and fifty Catalan forges in existence in northern New Jersey, many of them blown by the trompe, or water blast.

1803

"Hopewell," the first furnace in Ohio, was started by Daniel Eaton. It stood on the west side of Yellow Creek, about $1\frac{1}{4}$ miles from the junction of that stream with the Mahoning River, in the township of Poland, Mahoning County.

1814

Pierre Berthier published in France an important paper on the successful application of the waste gas from the blast furnace to various uses.

1816

The first wire suspension bridge in the United States, and probably in the world, was thrown across the Schuylkill River, near the Schuylkill Falls in Philadelphia. It was for foot passengers only, and not more than eight were allowed to be on the footway at one time. Wire was used to replace chain which had failed on two earlier bridges at this place.

1819

The first run of coke iron produced in America was made at Bear Furnace, Armstrong County, Pa., 86 years after the introduction of coke in England. The first experiment in America with the use of raw bituminous coal in the blast furnace was also made at Bear Furnace the same year. The furnace was built to use coke with a cold blast. It was blown by steam power, but the blast was too weak to be successful.

1820

The first rail rolling mill was started, and the development of the wrought-iron rail began with the granting of a patent by the English Government to John Birkenshaw, of the Bedlington Iron Works, for several forms of rolled edge rails. These rails were rolled in lengths of 15 to 18 feet, and were held in cast-iron chairs. They were fish-bellied in shape in imitation of the old cast-iron rails, and were called jumpers because of the irregular way they left the rolls. Mr. Birkenshaw proposed to weld the ends of the rails, but there is no record of this having been done.

The first iron ship that ever went to sea was the "Aaron Manby," built by the Horseley Company, near Birmingham, and put together in London. She made her first passage between London and Paris in the year 1820.

1827

The manufacturers of iron in the United States agitated and secured tariff protection at this time.

Many experiments in smelting with anthracite were made about this time. As cold blast was used, the experiments failed. But it was found possible to use part anthracite and part charcoal or coke, and this was done both by Peter Ritmer in Perry County, Pa., and in France, at the Vizille furnace.

1828

James Beaumont Neilson, then manager of the gas works of the city of Glasgow, Scotland, invented the hot blast; that is, the idea of heating the air to be used for combustion in forges, furnaces, etc. His patent was tried in 1829 at the Clyde Iron Works blast furnaces, and effected a reduction in the weight of coal required to be converted into coke and used to make a ton of iron from 8 tons 1¼ cwts. to 5 tons 3¼ cwts., although the blast was only heated in the original apparatus to some 300° F. Up to the time of the introduction of the hot blast, the output of an ordinary blast furnace would not average over 25 to 30 tons per week.

1829

John Laird introduced iron as a shipbuilding material by the construction in 1829 of a lighter 60 feet long, and in 1833 of a paddle steamer, the "Lady Lansdowne," of 148 tons burden. It was soon seen that iron ships could be made of the same capacity as wooden ones, but of half the weight.

1830

The production of pig iron in the United States this year was 165,000 tons. The production of bar iron was some 96,621 tons. There were then 14 steel furnaces in the country with a total capacity sufficient to produce about 1,600 tons of steel annually.

The water tuyere was invented and first used by John Condie, an English artisan, being found necessary when the hot blast was applied. For many years these tuyeres were made of cast iron, square outside, a hole in each outer corner closed with a wood plug, in two of which holes were bored and the water pipes secured with wood wedges.

Robert L. Stevens, president of the Camden and South Amboy Railroad Company, invented T-rails. He induced the Dowlais ironworks, at Dowlais, Glamorganshire, Wales, to roll the rails for him, and some were laid on his road the next year. Mr. Stevens also designed the hook headed spike, practically the railroad spike of today, and the "iron tongue," which has been developed into the fish plate and angle bar. The first T-rails weighed 36 pounds per yard; the second lot, 42 pounds.

1833

Dr. Frederick W. Geissenhainer, a Lutheran clergyman of New York City, was granted a patent for a "new and useful improvement in the manufacture of iron and steel by the application of anthracite coal." He used a strong blast, preferably heated. He made his invention late in 1830 or early in 1831 and filed his patent application in September, 1831. His work preceded any smelting with anthracite in Wales. The patent was sold by his executors after his death in 1838 to George Crane of Yniscedwyn, Wales,

Dr. Clark, professor of chemistry in the University of Aberdeen, Scotland, is quoted by Fairbairn as follows, to show the benefits wrought by hot blast up to this time.

"In 1829 the weekly produce of three furnaces, cold air and coke being used, was 110 tons, 14 cwts.; and the average of coal to one ton of iron was 8 tons 1 cwt.

"In 1830 the weekly produce of three furnaces, coke and air at 300°F. being used, was 162 tons, 2 cwts.; and the average of coal to one ton of iron was reduced to 5 tons, 3 cwts.

"In 1833 the weekly produce of four furnaces, raw coal and air heated to 600°F. being used, was 245 tons; and the average of coal to one ton of iron was reduced to 2 tons, 5 cwts. at the Clyde ironworks."

1834

Swank states that "the first practical application of the hot blast to the manufacture of pig iron in this country was made at Oxford furnace, in New Jersey, in 1834, by William Henry, the manager. The waste heat at the tymp passed over the surface of a nest of small cast iron pipes, through which the blast was conveyed to the furnace. The temperature was raised to 250°F. and the product of the furnace was increased about ten per cent. In 1835 a hot blast oven, containing cast-iron arched pipes, was placed on the top of the stack by Mr. Henry and heated by the flame from the tunnel head. By this means the temperature of the blast was raised to 500°F. The fuel used was charcoal."

1836

F. H. Oliphant, of Fayette County, Pa., made a quantity—probably over one hundred tons—of coke iron at his furnace called Fairchance, near Uniontown, but went back to the use of charcoal in his blast furnace because of the higher price he could secure for his charcoal iron.

Dr. Geissenhainer built the Valley Furnace on Silver Creek in Schulykill County, Pa., and smelted iron, using anthracite only as fuel, with hot blast of 2¾ to 3½ pounds pressure to the square inch. He had done this on a small scale five years earlier in New York City.

1837

The first successful manufacture of pig iron with anthracite and hot blast in England and Wales was accomplished by George Crane at Yniscedwyn, Wales.

The first successful use of coke in the blast furnace in the United States was at Lonaconing, Allegheny County, Md.

Sir William Fairbairn built a riveting machine, at his works in London, with which two men and a boy in one hour did the work that formerly took three men and a boy twelve hours. *A strike of boilermakers had suggested to Fairbairn the desirability of mechanical riveting.*

1838

Joseph Baughman, Julius Guitau, and Henry High, of Reading, Pa., built a small water power blast furnace at Mauch Chunk, to test thoroughly the smelting of iron with anthracite. Late in the previous year they had made some experiments in an old furnace of the Lehigh Coal and Navigation Company at Mauch Chunk, using 80 per cent of anthracite, which indicated success. Their blowing apparatus was two wood cylinders, 6 feet in diameter by 11 inch stroke. The furnace was $21\frac{1}{2}$ feet high, $5\frac{1}{2}$ feet bosh. They produced about $1\frac{1}{2}$ tons of iron per day with the blast heated to about 400°F., about seven hundred cubic feet of blast per minute being required.

1839

The first successful blast furnace use of anthracite in the United States was at the Pioneer furnace at Pottsville, Pa., which was blown in October 19, 1839, by Benjamin Perry and made about 28 tons of foundry iron a week. This furnace had been built by William Lyman, of Boston, and associates, under the auspices of Burd Patterson of Pottsville.

1840

Henry Burden, of Troy, N. Y., invented and patented the rotary squeezer for working puddled iron free of slag.

1841

Previous to the tariff act of September 11, rails were admitted into the United States free of duty; but after the passage of this act, and the more comprehensive act of 1842, capitalists began to prepare for the manufacture of heavy rails. It was not until early in 1844 that the actual making of heavy rails was started in this country.

The manufacture of Connellsville coke was commenced in western Pennsylvania.

1842

The first blast furnace in the United States to draw off unburned furnace gas for use by burning under steam boilers according to the idea introduced by Faber du Faur, of Wasseralfingen, Germany, was the Greenwood, in Orange County, N. Y. C. E. Detmold, of New York, as agent for Faber du Faur, patented this method in the United States in this year.

The commercial history of Connellsville coke began in 1842, when two small barges loaded with coke were floated down the Monongahela and Ohio rivers to Cincinnati where they were disposed of only with great difficulty and at a loss. The foundry men who secured this coke, however, found it so satisfactory that they later went to Connellsville, at considerable inconvenience, to secure further supplies.

1844

The first discovery by white men of iron ore in the Lake Superior region was made on September 16, 1844, near the eastern end of Teal Lake, in northern Michigan, by William A. Burt, a deputy surveyor of the general government.

1846

William Kelly discovered the pneumatic process of making malleable iron from pig iron. He and his brother bought the Suwannee Iron Works, near Eddyville, Ky., where they had about three hundred negro slaves, but imported Chinese, as they were opposed to slavery. They were the first employers to bring in Chinese labor in any numbers. Kelly noticed one day, while watching the finery fire, that the iron was actually heated by the blast of air at a point where there was no charcoal. The next week he publicly demonstrated the idea, converting some pig into steel and then making a horseshoe and shoeing a horse with the metal. The process must have been used by Kelly to some extent, for it is stated that some of the metal was used in boilers for steamboats on the rivers.

1849

Two anthracite furnaces were built at Durham in Bucks County, Pa., in 1848 and 1849, successors of the charcoal furnaces of 1727-89.

1850

The first shipment—about five tons—of iron ore was sent out from the Lake Superior region by A. L. Crawford, of Newcastle, Pa. Some of this ore was run down into blooms and rolled into bar iron.

1853

The first use of Lake Superior ore in a blast furnace in Pennsylvania occurred in this year, when about 70 tons, brought from Erie by canal at great expense, were used in the Sharpsville and Clay furnaces, in Mercer County.

The annihilation of the Turkish fleet at Sinope first drew general attention to the necessity of protecting war vessels from shell fire. The development of the naval shell gun thus led to the actual use of armor.

1854

Chenot took out his patent for making iron sponge by a direct method, reducing the ore by means of CO gas. He actually made steel at the works of Bageney & Company, near Paris.

The invention of Samuel Lucas (U. S. Pat. No. 1730), for converting bar iron and ore in one operation into steel, attracted much attention at that time. This was a cementation process, and both bar iron and ore were converted into steel by a carbonizing agent in the converting furnace.

In this year Henry Bessemer started his investigation with a view to producing an improved quality of iron for guns. This grew out of trials of his invention of a method of producing rotation of an elongated projectile when fired from a smooth-bore gun and with an enlarged powder chamber, necessitating great strength in the metal.

Sir Lowthian Bell started the Clarence Iron Works, near Middlesbrough, England.

1855

The output of anthracite iron in the United States for the first time exceeded that made with charcoal as fuel. At this time there were less than one hundred coke ovens in all Western Pennsylvania.

On March 6th the American Iron Association was organized. In 1864 (Nov. 16) its name was changed to the American Iron and Steel Association, which it retained, with headquarters in Philadelphia, until the death of Dr. Swank in 1914, when it was amalgamated with the American Iron and Steel Institute, with headquarters in New York, of which Judge E. H. Gary was for many years president.

The publication of the "Hardware Man's Newspaper" was commenced in the Summer of this year by John Williams in Middletown, N. Y. The name was changed to the "Iron Age" five years later and in 1868 Mr. Williams sold the paper to his son David.

The world's production of pig iron was estimated by Abram S. Hewitt to have amounted to seven million tons in this year.

The first 30-foot rails rolled in this country are claimed to have been rolled at the Cambria Ironworks, at Johnstown, in this year. There being no demand for them, they were used in the tracks of the Cambria Iron Company.

The Niagara Suspension Bridge was built by the firm of J. A. Roebling in the years 1852-1855. There was a long span of 821 feet, 245 feet above the river. There were four suspension cables, each 15 inches in diameter, and composed of seven strands containing 520 parallel wires, that is, 3640 No. 9 wires in each cable. The stiffening girder was constructed chiefly of timber, but was replaced with a long iron girder in 1880. The bridge was taken down in 1896-1897 and replaced with a steel arch bridge.

THE STEEL AGE

1856

This was a notable year in the development of iron and steel manufacture. Henry Bessemer, later knighted for his accomplishments, read his first important paper before the Cheltenham meeting of the British Association for the Advancement of Science, in August. In this paper he described his pneumatic process of making steel. His experimental apparatus had succeeded in converting a charge of seven cwts. of Bleanhaven iron into malleable iron a few days before he read that paper. Great excitement was created by this paper, and Bessemer was paid £27,000 for licenses within a month.

1857

The first Bessemer rail was rolled at Dowlais, Glamorganshire, Wales, in 1857, the rolls being driven by an engine which had been built in 1830 and was still running 1905. The rail was put into use on the main line of the Midland Railroad at Derby, England.

The first Michigan iron ore railway was completed. It extended from Marquette, on Lake Superior, to mines on the Marquette range. Another pioneer "ore line" about the same time, was the Catasauqua & Fogelsville line, put in operation by David Thomas, for supplying his furnaces at Catasauqua.

1858

The first pig iron produced in the Lake Superior region was made by Stephen R. Gay, in a small experimental furnace on Dead River, about three miles northwest of Marquette.

1860

Swank gives the following interesting statistical data: The production of pig iron in the United States was 821,223 tons; iron ore production was 2,401,485 tons. The production of steel was 11,838 tons; and there were 30,626 miles of railroad in operation in the United States. There were about two hundred Catalan forges or bloomeries south of the Ohio and Potomac rivers which made bar iron directly from the ore, many of them being blown by the trompe.

CIVIL WAR PERIOD

1861

The use of steel fire boxes for locomotives began on the Pennsylvania Railroad, this being the first use of steel for that purpose. The first steel used was of English manufacture which was found to be too hard and cracked in service; but in the next year, homogeneous steel of American manufacture was tried in locomotives Nos. 231 and 232, and worked successfully.

1862

The first steel rails used in the United States were imported from England by Philip S. Justice & Company, of Philadelphia and London. In this year J. Edgar Thomson, then president of the Pennsylvania Railroad, ordered a trial lot of 100 tons at $150 gold per ton. These were high carbon, crucible steel, and many broke in the cold weather, but the remaining ones withstood wear very well.

1863

The works of the Bethlehem Iron Company turned out its first product in this year; its first blast furnace was blown in January 4th; puddle furnaces began operations July 27th; first rails were rolled September 26th.

1865

In February, Alexander L. Holley was successful at Troy, N. Y., in producing Bessemer steel at experimental works which he had constructed for his company. Control of Bessemer's steel patents in the United States had been secured by John F. Winslow, John A. Griswold, and Alexander L. Holley, all of Troy, N. Y., the previous year.

THE STEEL AGE (Continued)

1867

American-made Bessemer steel rails first began to compete with iron rails.

The first steel rails ever rolled commercially in the United States, in the way of regular business, were rolled by the Cambria Iron Company, Johnstown, Pa., from ingots made by the Pennsylvania Steel Company, at Steelton.

1868

The first bell and hopper on an American blast furnace was put on the Merion anthracite furnace in Eastern Pennsylvania. The bell at first was too large and gave much trouble.

John Player, of England, introduced his iron hot blast stove into the United States. Mr. Player personally superintended the erection of the first of his stoves in this country at the anthracite furnace of J. B. Moorhead & Company, West Conshohocken, Pa.

1869

The output of coke and bituminous iron for the first time exceeded the production of charcoal iron.

1870

The production of various iron and steel commodities in the United States was as follows, according to figures given in the "Mineral Industry."

	Long Tons
Iron ore	5,302,952
Pig iron	1,865,000
Steel (all kinds)	68,750
Iron rails	523,214
Bessemer steel rails	30,357
Open-hearth steel	1,339

1872

Sir I. Lowthian Bell published his first important book, the "Chemical Phenomena of Iron Smelting." This had previously been published in the Iron and Steel Institute Journal.

1873

About this time the necessity of chemical control of operations in iron and steel metallurgy was being more generally recognized. A. L. Holley contributed a paper to the American Institute of Mining Engineers advocating the use of chemical analysis as well as physical testing to determine the character of steel required for specific uses. A chemist was employed at the Lucy furnaces and this innovation brought about excellent results. The Pennsylvania Steel Company at Harrisburg bought iron with chemical requirements, chief of which was phosphorus below .1 per cent.

1877

In the United States more rails were made of iron than of steel up to this year, and after this date the production of iron rails declined rapidly.

1878

The manufacture of rails from open-hearth steel was successfully commenced in this year. About 26 per cent of the open-hearth steel then made went into rails.

Use of coke as a furnace fuel had been increasing, but this year it was observed that coke had invaded producing districts heretofore exclusively using anthracite. In this year, for the first time, more iron was made with bituminous coal and coke than with anthracite and charcoal combined.

1886

About this year iron skeleton construction for office and other buildings was first used. Chicago was especially prominent in the early developments of this type of construction.

The first experiments in the United States with a basic hearth were conducted at the works of the Otis Steel Company, Cleveland, Ohio. Two years later regular and commercial operations were carried on at Homestead, Pa., while Steelton, Pa., followed soon after.

Last Charcoal furnace operated in the Lehigh Valley, Pa., was abandoned.

1895

A pig casting machine was patented by E. A. Uehling. This machine was developed for the continuous or intermittent casting of blast furnace metal into permanent iron molds. One of these machines was put in operation at the Lucy furnaces, Pittsburgh, for casting, conveying, and automatically loading blast furnace metal into freight cars in 1896.

1897

Thomas A. Edison erected a magnetic ore concentrating works in New Jersey, but it was not a commercial success.

1899

The world's production of pig iron was 39,410,000 tons, of which the United States produced 34.6%, the United Kingdom 23.6%, and Germany and Luxemburg 20.7%.

THE TWENTIETH CENTURY

1900

Mr. Stead reported results of his study of the condition of phosphorus in iron and steel. The study of various alloys of iron and steel was very vigorously prosecuted during this year.

1901

The Lackawanna Steel Company moved from Scranton, Pa., to Buffalo, N. Y., and added two large modern blast furnaces. The continuous Metal Refining Company, owning the Talbot process, passed under the same control as the Lackawanna Company.

1907

This was a record year from the standpoint of tonnage production in iron and steel in the United States. The total production of iron ore was 52,955,070 gross tons; 25,781,361 gross tons of pig iron were produced. There was a sharp break in this prosperity, however, in October, the country suffering from a very severe panic.

1920

In the closing days of 1920 the billionth ton of Lake Superior iron ore was shipped, the movement for 1920 bringing total shipments from that district to 1,006,956,394 tons.

1924

Charles P. Perin, New York, predicted that the world's actual iron ore reserves would be exhausted in 76 years if the present rate of consumption were maintained. Col. Leonard P. Ayres, a Cleveland economist, put forward his theory that the business cycle could be measured by the rate of activity of the blast furnaces.

1925

A sample from the famed Pillar of Delhi was analyzed by Sir Robert Hadfield, but no definite conclusions concerning the reason for the remarkable preservation of the pillar through 1,600 years were reached.

The sample showed the following composition: Carbon, 0.08; silicon, 0.046; sulphur, 0.006; phosphorus, 0.114; manganese, nil; and nitrogen 0.030 per cent; total, 0.276 per cent; iron 99.700 per cent; total 99.976 per cent. The specific gravity was 7.81. Sir Robert gave his conclusions before the French Congress of Chemical Industries at Paris in October.

NORTHERN NEW YORK STATE AREA

1798

The first Catalan forge in Plattsburg, N. Y. was built.

1801

Levi Highbey and George Throop erected an iron works at Willsboro Falls, on Lake Champlain, N. Y.

In the same year, Liberty Newman erected iron works at the upper falls in Ticonderoga, N. Y.

During this same period, we find records indicating the erection of a rolling mill on the Boquet River near Essex, N. Y. These plates were shipped to a nail factory in Vermont.

1802

One of the oldest iron works in Essex County was established at New Russia, N. Y. It was repeatedly rebuilt and operated until about 1866. The ore used here was obtained from the New Russia mine, situated a half mile from the works. A part of the ore was also obtained from the Fisher Hill Ore Bed.

1803

William Bailey erected a forge on the Chateaugay River about five miles below the outlet of Lower Chateaugay Lake, N. Y., which was operated for a few years. He probably obtained his ore from an old opening known as the Prall Vein. Its location and description are identical with 81 mine, Chateaugay Ore Bed.

1806

At Ferronia, N. Y., in the Town of Ausable, what is known as the Arnold Iron Mine was discovered by Samuel Baker.

1809

Archibald McIntire erected iron works within the limits of the present town of North Elba, Essex County, N. Y. The ore used in the beginning was found nearby, but was soon abandoned in favor of ore from the Arnold bed in Clinton County.

Subsequent to the year 1809 extensive iron works were established in Wilmington on the west branch of the Ausable River. Ore, transported from the Palmer Hill mine, was used in the forges.

We also find some small forges located at Lower Jay, N. Y. The ore used here was also obtained from the Palmer Hill mine.

1815

A rolling mill was constructed and operations commenced in 1816 by the Keeseville Rolling and Slitting Mill Company of Keeseville, N. Y. The principal product of the company was the manufacture of nail-plate which was subsequently cut into strips for the manufacture of horse shoe nails.

1822

Major James Dalliba, in connection with John D. Dickenson of Troy, erected the first furnace at Port Henry. The ore used was obtained from a vein near the furnace. The iron made was shipped to Troy, N. Y., until 1827 when the production of pig iron was abandoned and the works turned to the manufacture of stoves and hollow-ware.

1823

The Chateaugay Ore Body, at what is now Lyon Mountain, N. Y., was supposed to have been discovered by a trapper named Collins.

1824

The Peru Iron Company, located in the Ausable Valley of New York, was organized with a capital of $200,000.00, operating forges and rolling mills along the river.

About this same time, Zephaniah Palmer, a surveyor from the vicinity of Ausable Forks, N. Y., discovered iron ore outcroppings. Ore from this mine was sold mainly to the Peru Iron Company; however, being lower in metallic iron than the Arnold ore, it required concentration. In 1837 a separator was built on the Ausable River at Clintonville, N. Y.

1826

The first forge in the town of Saranac, N. Y., on the Saranac River, was built by Hull, Hopper and Baker. The ore was obtained from the Arnold Ore Bed, located about fourteen miles away.

In the subsequent years it was rebuilt, new machinery installed and it became one of the largest and most efficient forges in the Adirondacks. The ore used was obtained from the Tremblay mine, near Redford, N. Y.

Two blast furnaces were finished and put in operation at Clintonville, N. Y. They were charged with wood and charcoal, and blown by cold blast. Ironware as well as pig iron was made here, the castings being poured direct from the furnace. In January, 1828, a cable factory, manufacturing large ship anchors and iron cables, was erected.

ORE SEPARATOR IN THE ADIRONDACKS, EARLY PART OF 19TH CENTURY

1827

Approximately three miles west of Essex Village, N. Y., Gould, Ross and Low erected and operated a rolling mill for the fabrication of bars and iron plates from blooms.

1828

A four-fire forge was built six miles west of the Lake on Putnam's Creek, near Crown Point, N. Y. A good grade of iron was evidently manufactured at this plant, for records indicate an order received from the government for a large quantity of this iron, which was to be fabricated into chain cables.

The first forge at Morrisonville, N. Y. was built by Heman Smith and Josiah Wilcox. However, the freshet of 1830 destroyed it, ending the iron business at Morrisonville.

Burt and Vanderwarker erected a four-fire forge at Ausable Forks, N. Y. They procured their ore from the Palmer Hill mine, located two miles north of the village.

1831

J. & J. Rogers began making iron at Black Brook, N. Y., hauling the ore for their forges from Arnold Hill.

1832

A mining company of ten men was formed and purchased what is known as the Averill ore beds, located in the vicinity of Dannemora, N. Y.; but the Company did nothing to develop them at this time.

1833

Heman and Cyrus Cady built a forge at Cadyville, N. Y., located a few miles above Morrisonville on the Saranac River.

1836

Sailly & Averill erected a forge on the Saranac River between the villages of Morrisonville and Cadyville, N. Y. In 1837 Sailly & Averill's forge was destroyed by fire. In its stead they erected a forge consisting of two fires and a hammer in one end, run by Mr. Sailly, and two fires and a hammer in the other end, run by Mr. Averill. In connection with this four-fire forge, they had a large rolling mill for making wagon axles, etc.

1837

The Rogers began making iron at Ausable Forks, N. Y. During this same period, iron manufacture flourished throughout this valley at Wilmington, New Sweden and Clintonville. Near the Arnold ore bed was the two-fire Batty forge, and above that the Etna blast furnace, operated under the name of the Peru Smelting Company.

ROLLING MILL IN THE ADIRONDACKS, MIDDLE OF THE 19TH CENTURY

During this period, Goulding and Peabody erected a foundry, employing about sixty men, casting the principal machinery for all the forges, saw mills, grist mills, in the valleys of Ausable and Saranac, at Keeseville, N. Y. They used the Port Henry, N. Y. pig iron.

In subsequent years the iron-workers in this valley manufactured such things as wire and horseshoe nails. One Daniel Dodge invented, received a patent for, and manufactured the first machine for turning out, mechanically, forged horseshoe nails.

The Merriams, father and son, erected and operated the Stower forge at Lewis, N. Y., located about five miles from Elizabethtown, N. Y. The forge contained three fires, and used ore procured from Moriah.

1841

The Caldwell mine, the first mine opened in the Saranac Valley, was operated by Cashman. During the period between 1841 and 1844 the owners of the property erected a separator and a four-fire forge. This mine is located at Clayburg, N. Y., and is now owned by the Chateaugay Ore and Iron Company.

Peter Tremblay discovered and opened the Tremblay mine. This mine, which produced a good grade of ore, was located one mile south of Redford, on the south side of the Saranac River, and is now owned by the Chateaugay Ore and Iron Company.

1842

Charles K. Averill and F. L. C. Sailly bought up the interests of the Averill ore beds at Dannemora, N. Y. They opened the mine, built a separator, and did a lively business for a number of years. The business was subsequently conducted by Burton, Chittenden & Company and finally abandoned.

The first iron ore separator using water jigs in the town of Moriah, near Mineville, N. Y., was built by Eliphalet Hall.

1844

The first forge at Russia, N. Y. was established by Spaulding & Parsons.

1845

Hammond & Bogue erected a furnace at Crown Point, N. Y. The ore was obtained from the bed owned by the firm, located about a mile from the works. The product was shipped to the Bessemer Steel Works at Troy, N. Y.

On the north side of the Saranac River, at Plattsburg, N. Y., Hobart & Hedges built a six-fire Catalan forge, which in 1873 was replaced by a six-fire Catalan forge, erected by Mr. Christopher Norton.

A forge was built at Russia, N. Y., by Jackson & Stearns. The ownership of this forge subsequently changed hands many times. Among the owners we find in 1856, the Company of Lee, Sherman & Witherbee of Port Henry, N. Y. In 1864, it came under control of Parsons & Company of Saranac, N. Y. In 1872, it was obtained by Andrew Williams and C. F. Norton; and in 1878 it became the possession of the firm of Williams & Moffitt.

1846

A six-fire forge was erected at Valley Forge, N. Y., a half mile south of Elizabethtown and about eight and one-half miles from Westport, N. Y. This forge obtained its ore from the Burt mine, a distance of about ten miles.

The Westport forge, located about four miles from Westport on the Boquet river, contained three fires and one hammer. It worked Moriah ore, transported by land from Westport. It was owned by W. P. and P. D. Merriam.

1847

The original Port Henry furnace was demolished and a larger one built. The ore was obtained from the Cheever bed, located nearby.

1848

Francis H. Jackson erected, at a cost exceeding $100,000.00, the Westport Furnace. It was located in the North West bay, about one mile from Westport village. Its product was pig iron and was made from ore from the Cheever bed.

Messrs. McIntyre, Robertson and Henderson built a blast furnace at Tahawus, Essex County, N. Y., for smelting titaniferous iron ore from the immense deposits located there. The old furnace still stands.

1851

A forge was built at Elsinore, N. Y., by Moore and Gillman.

1852

Witherbee, Sherman & Company, of Mineville, N. Y., began experiments with magnetic separation in this year, but it was not until the '80s that magnetic separation became commercial.

1853

It is interesting to note that, at Port Henry, the old charcoal furnaces were repaired and anthracite was substituted for charcoal as fuel. The ores used were obtained from both the Cheever and Barton beds.

1854

One of the blast furnaces completed in this year at Port Henry, N. Y., is said to have been the first furnace ever made completely incased in an iron shell. It was 46 feet high with a 15 foot bosh.

1861

The Fairbanks Mine, on top of the mountain back of Dannemora, N. Y., was opened by Jason Fairbanks. It was worked some by him, and subsequently by Andrew Williams and by the State; but it proved too lean and inaccessible, finally being abandoned.

1862

A new forge was built at Plattsburg, N. Y., to replace the Sailly & Averill plant. They manufactured slabs for boiler plates, blooms, and refined billets.

1863

The Ausable Horse-Nail Company was formed, with a capital of $40,-000.00, at Ausable Forks, N. Y. They began operations with ten machines and sold during the first year one hundred tons of nails.

1864

At Irondale, about one mile above the Forks of the Saranac River, Peter Tremblay built a forge and separator. He used ore from the mine bearing his name.

The Ticonderoga Iron Company, under the direction of W. E. Calkins, erected a six-fire forge at the Lower Falls, about two miles from the steamboat landing at Ticonderoga, N. Y. The ore used was shipped from Port Henry, N. Y.

1865

The Fletcherville furnace was blown in. It was located about eight miles northwest of Port Henry. It was owned by S. H. and J. G. Witherbee and F. P. Fletcher. The ore was obtained from the company's mines located nearby. A large proportion of the iron produced here was used in the Bessemer works at Troy, N. Y.

1867

Thomas F. Witherbee was one of the first furnace managers in the United States to use the chemical laboratory in connection with the regular operation of the furnace. He started this practice when operating the Fletcherville charcoal blast furnace, about this year, near Mineville, N. Y.

1868

At Irona, in the town of Altona, N. Y., Asa Reynolds built a four-fire forge. The ore used at first was transported from the Port Henry and Arnold Hill mines, but later brought from the vicinity of Lower Chateaugay Lake.

Foot, Mead, Waldo and Weed made a contract with Edmund Rogers, son of Lloyd N. Rogers, for the working of the Chateaugay ore beds, and began the development of the properties.

BOWEN AND SIGNOR'S IRON WORKS, SARANAC, N. Y., 1871
THE ORE BED NOW OWNED BY CHATEAUGAY

1869

Frank Palmer erected a five-fire forge at Altona, N. Y. Like the Reynolds forge, Palmer at first obtained his ore from Port Henry and Arnold Hill, subsequently changing to that of the Chateaugay Ore Bed.

1870

The top of the Fletcherville blast furnace near Mineville, N. Y., was closed with a four-foot bell and hopper. This was one of the first furnaces in the United States to adopt a closed top. Anthracite was tried because of a shortage of charcoal. The furnace was raised to a height of 60 feet and the tunnel head increased to eight feet diameter.

1871

Bowen and Signor obtained ownership of the Hull, Hopper and Baker forge in Saranac Lake, N. Y. on the Saranac River. The forge was improved and enlarged, making it one of the most up-to-date in the Valley.

1874

A new rolling mill, nail factory and foundry were built at Ausable Forks, N. Y., by J. & J. Rogers.

Operations of a ten-fire Catalan forge were begun by Pope, Williams & Company of Plattsburg, N. Y., at Belmont, N. Y., on the Chateaugay River, just below the outlet of Lower Chateaugay Lake. Ore was obtained for the forges from the famous Chateaugay ore beds.

A dam was built at the outlet of Lower Chateaugay Lake, furnishing water power for operating the Catalan forges at Belmont, N. Y.

1876

The first set of Siemens-Cowper-Cochrane fire brick hot blast stoves erected in this country was built at one of the Crown Point furnaces in Essex County, N. Y.

1877

On March 15th, the iron works at Belmont, N. Y. were bought and operated by the Chateaugay Ore and Iron Company, of Lyon Mountain, N. Y., which was also the owner of the Chateaugay Ore Bed.

1883

At this time there were about 277 forges in the Champlain district, Northern New York. They included 1171 forge fires, and produced nearly 44,000 tons in this calendar year. In 1890, the number of forges had been reduced to 14, with 102 fires. Their production in 1889 was only 12,397 net tons of blooms.

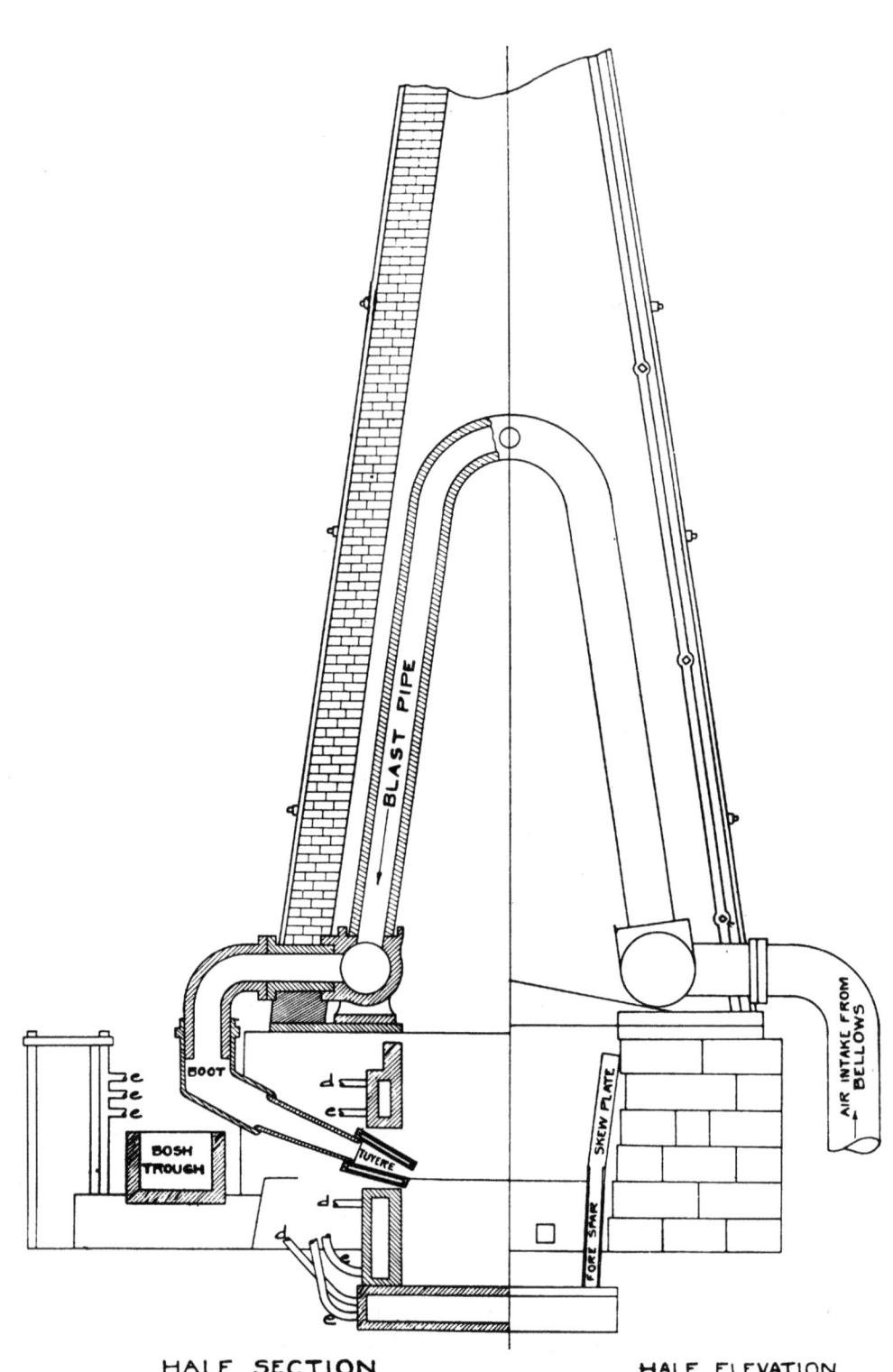

HALF SECTION HALF ELEVATION

THREE-PIPE BLOOMERY FORGE AT BELMONT, N. Y.
TYPICAL OF FORGES USED IN EARLY PART OF NINETEENTH CENTURY

1913
  The McIntyre Iron Company engaged in an extensive series of experiments to determine the feasibility of smelting titaniferous ores of the Sanford district in Essex County, N. Y.

1915
  At Port Henry, N. Y., Witherbee, Sherman & Company completed a new concentrating plant with a capacity for treating 1400 tons of crude ore in nine hours, the largest iron ore concentrator of its type in the world.

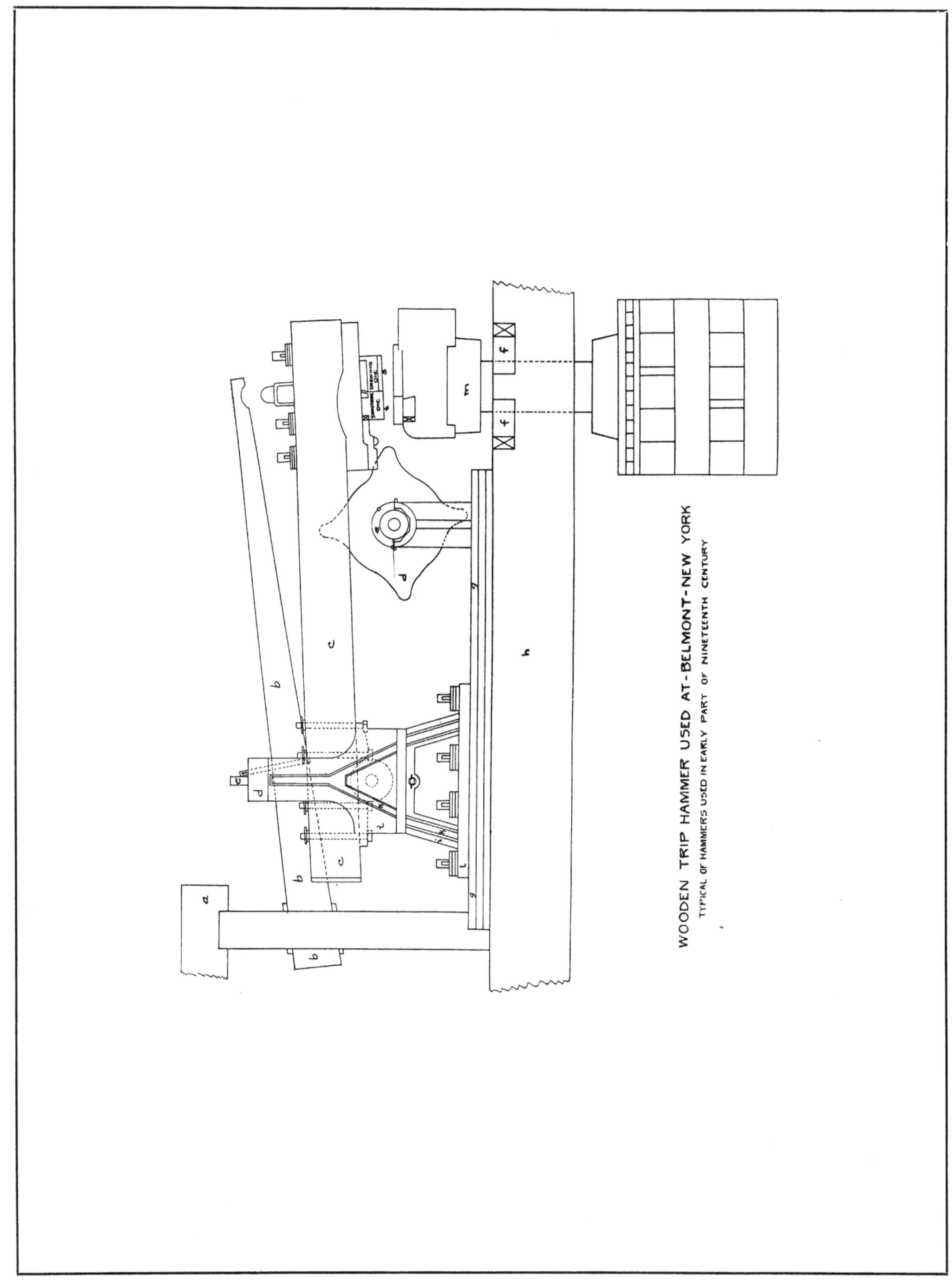

The Old Guide's Story
Trained in the great outdoors rather than in the school, guide Charles E. Merrill (1863-1935), had a real story to tell--the great epic of the struggles of the pioneers in the woods, the fight with the elements, and the joys and sorrows of a primitive mode of life.

$49.95

Hunting Adventures in the Northern Wilds
This is the personal journal of the hunting experiences of Samuel H. Hammond and his guide Joe Tucker in the unbroken paradise of the Adirondack Mountains in the mid 1800s.

$24.95

The Lost Prince
Did the little boy, the Dauphin who would have become Louis XVII, rightful king of France, survive the horrors of captivity in 1795? Was he spirited away from Paris to be raised by a Mohawk family in Caughnawage?

$24.95

The U.S. Campaign of 1813
From the early 19th century comes a history rich with heroic tales and epic battles as the early explorers wrestled civilizations out of the bare earth of North America.

$4.95

TEACH Services, Inc.
history.tsibooks.com
518.358.3494

Your source for books of local historical interest

Franklin County Family Album

This book contains over 300 rarely seen photographs of places and scenes of a bygone era of Franklin County, NY, including rare photographs of places in all nineteen towns and several villages. Franklin County was once stigmatized as "the Siberia of New York" because most of the territory was one great pine forest when first settled.

$49.95

*DVD now available for $19.95

Adirondack Lifestyles

This coffee-table style book packed full of old and interesting photographs will make the perfect addition to any historian's collection. This book contains approximately 300 photographs of people, places, and things local to the Adirondacks in the late 1800s to early 1900s.

$49.95

Place Names of Franklin County NY

This book's historical view of how each township's name was acquired is an entertaining and invaluable resource to not only researchers and genealogists, but also for the layman to read and enjoy.

$24.95

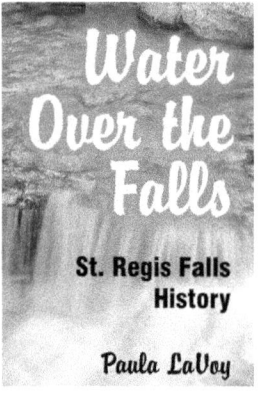

Water Over the Falls

St. Regis Falls was carved out of the Adirondack woods. Author Paula Lavoy has talked to old-timers who heard the local legends first hand from their ancestors. Unable to keep these wonderful vignettes to herself, she has compiled Water Over the Falls to share with others.

$24.95

Franklin Historical Review

Compilations of Vols. 1-5, 6-10 and 11-15.

These books offer tidbits of history, stories, photos and little known facts about, but not limited to, Malone, Chateaugay, Bellmont, St. Regis Falls, Brandon, West Bangor and Constable. Interesting topics and stories such as "old time railroading," "horse thieves," and "the case of the eccentric millionaire" are delved into. Available in hardback and paperback

Paperback $24.95 each
Hardcover $49.95 each

TEACH Services, Inc.
history.tsibooks.com
518.358.3494

www.ingramcontent.com/pod-product-compliance
Lightning Source LLC
Chambersburg PA
CBHW081838170426
43199CB00017B/2766